"I was shocked when I learned that m

had built his own airplane and then h
INVERTED is a great testimony of h
everything in pursuit of your loftiest … importance of keeping faith and family at the forefront when all seems to be lost."

—Jerry Falwell
President, Liberty University

"As someone who's been a part of the experimental world for a long time, I was glad to hear when another plane was completed, and to know that one of our own EAA Chapter 646 members was the proud builder. I'd had the privilege of talking with Chuck a few times during the building process, but until reading his book, I didn't realize all that he'd been through with his plane. *INVERTED* will be an encouragement to builders, pilots, and everyone who's ever faced adversity."

—Bob Barrows
Designer of the Bearhawk experimental plane

"There are times in our lives where God receives our full attention. When this occurs our relationship with Him grows as our finite mind attempts to understand His infinite mind. The result is a greater glimpse of His endless love and caring for us individually. Chuck provides us with a personal look into one of those times when the old saying "aviation is inherently dangerous" is proven true once again."

—John Marselus
Colonel (Ret.), USAF

"We've all read aircraft accident reports. What we seldom read is the personal aftermath from those accidents. This book is the whole story, from a landing accident to the lengthy recovery from serious injury, to the discovery of new meaning in life. The book is both deeply sincere and meaningful."

—Lauran Paine, Jr.
Retired military & airline pilot,
columnist for EAA *Sport Aviation,*
and author of *The Flying Life: Stories for the Aviation Soul*

"I enjoyed *INVERTED: Looking Back on Walking Away* from its first page, and was surprised when I found myself experiencing that old cliché 'couldn't put it down.' Among the book's many standout moments, Chuck's summary of the Wright brothers and early experimental flight is one of the best I've read, and he gives even a well-read enthusiast fresh insights into early aviation. He then masterfully walks us through the demanding long hours and years of building an experimental aircraft, and accurately portrays the immense joy of finally flying one's own creation. Chuck's heartbreaking crash is told objectively, and his months of rehabilitation give us a new appreciation of what the human spirit and body can overcome. Lastly, Chuck does every reader a huge service with his broad overview of 'lessons learned.' I wholeheartedly recommend this book to anyone—pilot, aircraft builder, adventure enthusiast, or simply those with an interest in human capability."

—Jeremiah D. Jackson, PhD
Author of *The Flight of the Feral Chihuahua, In Pursuit of the Round-Trip Transcontinental Speed Record,* and *Four Minutes: Surviving the Crash of an Experimental Airplane*

"This is more than just a story about a plane accident. It's a very readable description of experimental aviation, coupled with a candid account of severe injury, successful surgeries, and the personal lessons that can be learned—about yourself and God—through unexpected setbacks. It's not about what happens, but how we handle it when it does!"

—Dave Young
Brigadier General, USAF (Ret.),
Liberty University Assistant Provost
for Aeronautics Education

INVERTED

Chuck Hagerty

INVERTED

Looking Back on Walking Away

CJHSR Publishing Group

Published in the United States by CJHSR,
an imprint of the CJHSR Publishing Group,
a division of CaGNaC, Inc.

Library of Congress Control Number xxxxxxxxxxx

ISBN 978-0-9909013-0-3
eBook ISBN 978-0-9909013-2-7

Cover Design by Gerald Bergstrom

Manufactured in the United States of America

Printed in the United States by Morris Publishing
www.morrispublishing.com
Kearney, NE

For Gail

It is only with the heart that one can see rightly;
what is essential is invisible to the eye.

— Antoine de Saint-Exupéry

CONTENTS

PREFACE

CAN'T MOVE MY RIGHT HAND. MY NECK HURTS. THE JUNE SUN shone brightly as we hung upside down beside the runway of a small Pennsylvania airport.

Disoriented and dazed, I looked at my wife; her eyes were closed. *Lord, no!* Bright spots of blood seeped from shallow cuts on her face.

Slowly she opened her eyes, touched her cheek, and noticed the blood on her hand. "Am I disfigured?" she whispered.

Gathering my thoughts and focusing wasn't easy. "You'll be okay…we have to get out of here."

I hated myself for hurting her as gas fumes drifted into the cockpit.

Five months earlier, my new RV-7A experimental plane flew for the first time. What a high—the culmination of years of learning and hard work. The "RV grin" had been on my face for two days, and I was so proud.

Five weeks earlier, I completed the testing phase, and took a flight instructor friend flying. We were both grinning, and I felt even prouder.

Five hours earlier, my son Nathan went up with me for his first ride in our new plane. Good pictures, big smiles, shiny plane, and shiny pride.

Five minutes earlier, Gail and I were on final approach at Altoona-Blair County Airport. Family members waited; we were anxious to show off the plane.

Five seconds earlier: gusting winds, moment of distraction, flared high, bounced, landed hard, bent nose-wheel, skidded off runway, hit the dirt, and flipped the plane. *This can't be happening. My beautiful plane is wrecked, Gail and I are hurt, and my shining sense of pride is suddenly tarnished.*

Years of dreams, shattered in an instant.

Everyone talks about the highs and lows of life…the mountaintops and the valleys. Rick Warren prefers to compare life to a set of train tracks. The tracks run side by side: One rail represents the good in life, the other represents the bad, and there are no highs where everything is all good, just as there are no lows where everything is all bad. Good and bad things run parallel, and both are always present—they vary only in degree.

We would all prefer to avoid the trials, but they're always there—challenging us and trying to steal our joy, discourage us, or worse. Every day we assimilate the good with the bad, and our lives are molded through a combination of experiences and attitude. Viktor Frankl contemplated all this while suffering the horrors of a World War II concentration camp, and he concluded that in order for life to make sense, we must first find meaning in our tragedies.

Through the process of building an experimental airplane, learning to fly it, and then experiencing a life-altering crash, some extreme highs and lows were compressed into a relatively short span. This book was written because I endured nine months of inactivity and recovery, and putting the story on paper has been my way of dealing with those challenges.

I wouldn't have chosen to go through several of the things I'm about to share with you, but that's not the way life works. The "train" rolls on, and the following pages celebrate my discovery of meaning.

PART

I

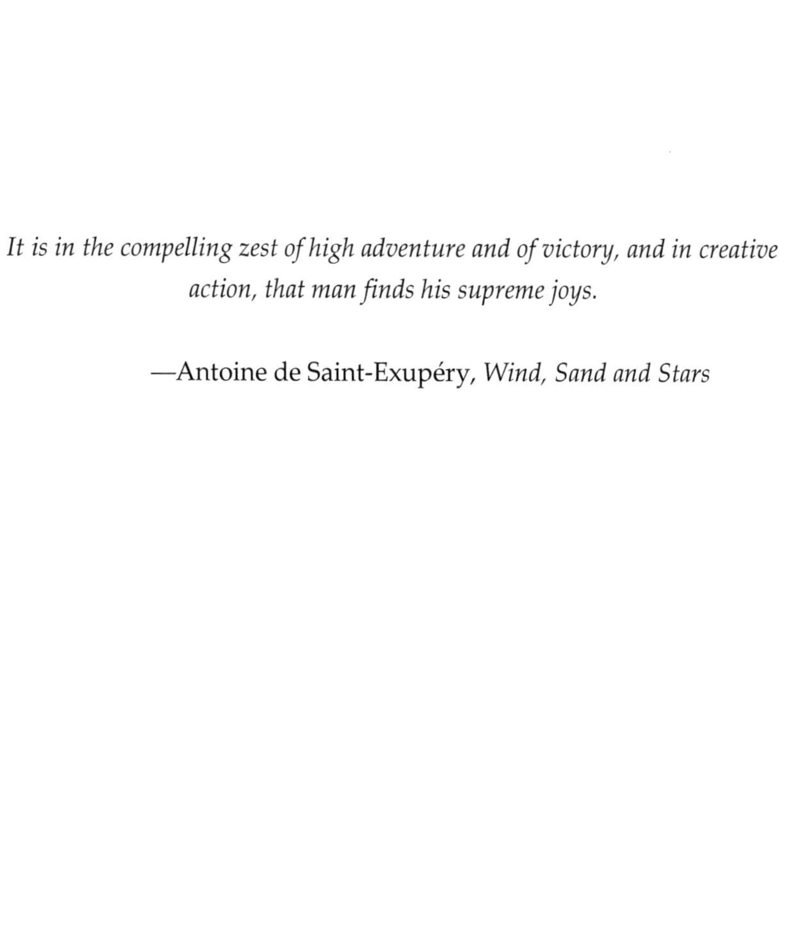

It is in the compelling zest of high adventure and of victory, and in creative action, that man finds his supreme joys.

—Antoine de Saint-Exupéry, *Wind, Sand and Stars*

One

First Flight

MY FIRST FLYING LESSON WAS TAKEN ON FEBRUARY 4, 1976. I was a nineteen-year-old college student living in Lynchburg, Virginia, and my flight instructor's name was Jeff Robinson. Tall, lanky, and only slightly older than I, Jeff was an exciting part of my life for about six months. He moved on to bigger flying venues soon after I obtained my license, and I haven't seen him now for almost forty years. Certain events and certain people, however, are imprinted forever on your brain, and that first flying lesson will be there until dementia takes over and I lose all cogent thought. I liked Jeff; he was a good instructor—methodical and exacting, but also patient. He could correct you without making you feel stupid.

Along with liking Jeff, I also liked that first flight. I say "first flight," but it really wasn't the first time I had ever flown. When I was around twelve years old, my family visited the American side of Niagara Falls. My dad was intrigued by helicopters, and when he saw that helicopter rides were available for a fee he considered reasonable, we all got to go flying—my father, my mother, me, my brother Dan (two years younger than I am) and my brother Rob (ten years younger).

The flight over the falls probably only lasted about ten or fifteen minutes, but man, was it ever exciting! Dust billowed up, the blades made a frightening noise, and the machine shook—a lot. I was scared to death. But somehow the excitement, the sensations, the uniqueness, and the view all made fear a price I was willing to pay. I loved it.

That was my one and only exposure to flying as a young person. I didn't hang out around an airport. Nobody in my immediate family was a pilot. I seldom read about planes and had assembled just a few plastic models. I could only identify a couple of military planes, and I couldn't have told you the difference between a Cessna and a Piper.

I did, however, know quite a bit about Ducati, Moto Guzzi, BMW, Harley, Honda, Yamaha, Suzuki, Kawasaki, and several other makes of motorcycles, thanks to the magazine *Cycle*. My parents bought a subscription for me when I was around ten, and I looked forward to each issue, reading it carefully from cover to cover. Two-wheeled sources of speed and thrills kept me occupied until I left for college. Then the bikes had to go, and all my efforts—and my money—went toward taking classes and working to pay for those classes. Life was busy, but boring.

That changed somewhere in the first semester of the 1975–76 school year. The small college I attended was investigating the possibility of starting an aviation program. Two different companies in town were vying for the school's business, and somehow I found out about this proposed program. Each of the companies offered a package that included forty hours of ground school and forty hours of flight time. I can't remember the exact cost, but the low bidder came in with an unbelievably low price. How could I not take advantage of such a good deal?

A few weeks after making this discovery, I attended an introductory meeting along with five or six other guys. We wouldn't be getting school credit for the program—it was officially independent of the school—but the offer was so appealing that each of us ended up signing papers to begin flight training. I don't remember if everyone in the group ultimately earned a private license or not, but I think most did.

As an interesting side note, the college was not able to get the aviation program up and running at that time. However, a number of years later they tried again, and the program has gone on to become one of the two largest Christian aviation schools in America. The school is Liberty University School of Aeronautics, and it is headed by retired USAF Brig. Gen. Dave Young. I'm quite pleased to have been an early part of a university aviation program that has gone on to become so successful.

Which brings us back to that first flying lesson.

Even though we weren't getting school credit, the flight program was going to follow the college's schedule. It was January 1976, and the second semester was starting. The first few weeks of the program kept us in the classroom, where we learned the names of numerous airplane parts and controls and where we also learned the rudimentary principles of flight and communication.

It wasn't long before I had completed the classroom portion and was ready to begin flying. February 4, 1976, was a sunny, cold Wednesday, and when I met Jeff at the Lynchburg airport I could see the Blue Ridge Mountains rising in the distance. I don't remember if it was morning or afternoon, but I do remember the smell of the plane. The aviation school used two Piper 140s that were several years old, and the smell was distinctive. It isn't a bad smell and yet it can't be called good either (unless you like to fly—then it's very good). I believe the odor comes from the electronic and mechanical devices in the instrument panel along with a mix of aviation gas and oil.

The pre-flight took awhile, since this was the first one I had ever done, and my instructor Jeff was a thorough guy. The inspection of the moveable exterior parts of the plane (such as the ailerons, elevators, rudder, and flaps) were all accompanied by Jeff's unhurried explanation of exactly how these parts affected the flight of the plane. Likewise, looking at tires, brakes, propeller, cowling attachments, antennae, wings, doors, vertical and horizontal stabilizer leading edges, pitot tube, static ports, lights, and the overall condition of the fuselage, all prompted a discussion on the importance of each part.

Eventually we reached Jeff's two favorite subjects—the oil and the gas, or "the lifeblood of the plane," as he liked to say. We inspected the amount of gas in each tank, made certain the gas caps were secured, checked for water in the fuel, and examined the oil dipstick, taking care to properly refasten the small access door on the cowling. Finally, we removed any chocks or tie-downs that were keeping the plane from moving. This almost religious ceremony was to be performed faithfully and with great solemnity; now was not the time to be inattentive or frivolous. Jeff made it clear that flying was serious business and that your life depended on your own diligence.

By now my heart was beating fast. The thrill of flying in a small craft for only the second time, along with the responsibility of operating the controls, was starting to hit hard. *Tell me again why I signed up for these lessons?* The classroom instruction for the past few weeks had been interesting, but things were about to get serious.

A Piper 140 is a low-wing plane, and you have to step up onto the wing in order to get in the cockpit. I clearly remember the feeling of stepping on the wing, easing down into the cabin, and taking my place for the first time in the left seat—the pilot's seat. It may have been winter, but my nervous chills weren't caused by the cold. Jeff showed me how to adjust the seat and position myself properly. The smell was already making its indelible impression in my memory, and I breathed it in deeply.

The cabin pre-flight checklist was followed just as methodically as the external checklist. All required FAA documentation was verified to be in the plane; the necessary aeronautical charts were placed within easy reach; the pin that kept the yoke from moving was removed; engine monitoring gauges were turned on and checked; fuel gauges were verified; flap operation was checked; and any meter that monitored flight time was reset to zero.

We're getting close. Jeff walked me through the engine-starting procedure, and after a few minutes the shout of "Clear prop!" was given, the propeller spun a couple times, and the engine roared to life. The plane was shaking, but probably not as much as I was! We checked the oil pressure and adjusted the radio as we waited for the oil temperature to come up to 100 degrees Fahrenheit. It didn't take long, and in what seemed like seconds, Jeff received permission to taxi to the active runway. *That guy in the tower really talks fast. I'm not totally sure what he said. It's going to take some time to learn this new language.*

We taxied to the end of the runway, where there was a paved area on the side with room for several planes. I steered the plane off to the side, and Jeff produced the pre-takeoff checklist: securing the doors, making certain the flight controls move freely, positioning the fuel selector valve, setting the mixture control to full rich, adjusting the elevator trim to neutral, turning the fuel pump on, setting the transponder to altitude, and then the best part…doing the "run-up."

The "run-up" is done to check the engine instruments, the magnetos, and the operation of the throttle. It involves increasing the engine rpm to 1,700 while stepping hard on the brakes—the plane shakes for about thirty seconds until the throttle is pulled back to idle. What a rush, and we hadn't even left the ground yet!

Now we're ready to fly, and this time, Jeff says, it's my turn to talk to the tower. *Are you kidding me? I barely understood him the last time!* Fortunately, I only needed to identify our plane and say that we were ready for takeoff; I think I did it correctly. Who knows? At this point my mind was already going 100 mph.

The tower gave us approval, and we taxied onto the center of the runway. Jeff wasn't controlling the plane but was instead telling me what to do. *I didn't think I'd actually be the one flying the plane right from the beginning!* "Ease the throttle all the way forward, smoothly, while keeping the elevator and ailerons level. Don't forget to push on the right rudder," said Jeff. That really didn't sound too hard, but I was still thankful to see that Jeff's hand was just below his yoke. He was ready to help if needed—good thing.

The plane started rolling down the runway, picking up speed, as I struggled to keep the nose pointed forward and the front wheel on the center line. We needed to reach about 60 knots before this thing would fly, and there's a lot to be done all at the same time. It reminded me of juggling chain saws—you have to concentrate, it's noisy, things vibrate, and if you make a mistake you'll probably get hurt. And there's something I forgot to mention...neither of us were wearing headsets. There was a speaker on the radio and a handheld microphone; that's how we communicated with that hard-to-understand guy in the tower. So along with the normal shaking, vibration, and bumpiness of a takeoff, it was *loud* in the cockpit.

Finally the airspeed reached 60 and Jeff motioned for me to pull the yoke back. The wheels left the ground, the little Piper climbed steadily into the sky, and I was actually flying a plane for the first time in my life. Are we having fun yet? You better believe it!

My pilot's logbook recorded that we flew for one hour, but I don't honestly remember all of it. I remember the takeoff, and then later, how large everything became as we were coming down for the landing. Oddly enough, I don't remember the actual landing. I do, however, remember very clearly that we stalled the plane several times during that first hour of instruction.

Now, a "stall" is probably not what you think it is. Most people assume that the engine quits during a stall, just as it sometimes does in a car. Nope, it's nothing like that.

A plane is able to fly because air is flowing smoothly over the wings at a fast enough rate to create lift. This is related to something called "Bernoulli's principle." However, if you raise the nose of the plane and change the angle of the wings so that air is not flowing smoothly anymore, then the wings will stop producing lift and the plane will stall. The textbooks say, "A stall is caused by the separation of airflow from the wing's upper surface." Simply put, *you're in a world of trouble because this plane won't fly much longer if you don't do something fast!* The only solution to a stall is to get the nose of the plane pointed down and the air flowing smoothly over the wings again—preferably quickly.

A stall can occur whether the plane is going fast or slow and whether the engine is at idle (a power-off stall) or wide open (a power-on stall). Of course, if the power's off and the plane's speed is slow, then the stall is smoother and the nose of the plane won't be pointed up very steeply. But if the power's on and the plane is going faster, you're in for a scary ride. Your stomach falls to your shoes and you're pressed deeply into your seat when the nose of the plane suddenly goes up sharply. You stay in that position as the speed of the plane starts to decrease. Then, as the flow of air over the wings slows down, the whole plane begins to shake and the "stall warning" siren blares loudly, telling you to do something now or this plane is going to quit flying. That's when you push the nose down—your stomach jams up into your chest—and you quickly go from a reclining position (staring at the clouds) to an "I'm falling forward out of the sky" position (looking at the ground). It's those sudden movements in any plane that can make you nauseous, and if you're prone to motion sickness you might find yourself getting queasy at this point.

Do you remember when I said earlier that I liked my instructor Jeff? Well, at this point I'm thinking that he's either trying to kill both of us, or he just doesn't want me to ever fly again. This was my first flying lesson and Jeff had me doing five or six of these things in a row. I never usually get nauseous but I just about lost it during the last one. Fortunately the stalls were at the end of the lesson and soon afterwards we headed back to the airport. Maybe that's the real reason I don't remember much of my first landing.

However, just like the first time I flew in that helicopter over Niagara Falls, the excitement, the sensation, the uniqueness, and the view were all more powerful than fear, and I was back for my second lesson in two days. I still didn't like a power-on stall very much, but eventually I learned to do them safely.

In twenty-three days I did my first solo flight. Anyone who has ever taken flying lessons will always remember that first solo. After ten to fifteen hours of instruction, you've gained some confidence and you're controlling the plane completely on your own, but the security blanket, your instructor, is still in the plane with you. When he/she gets out and tells you to do three "touch and gos" by yourself, it's a whole new ball game! You either do it right or you have a problem...maybe a life-threatening problem. The first thing you notice as soon as you take off is that the plane feels lighter and handles differently. Your instructor probably weighed between 140 and 200 pounds, and in a small plane, that's a big weight difference. I could feel it as soon as I took off…the plane was climbing faster than ever before, and the seriousness of what I was doing hit me immediately. I had to continually wipe my hands on my pants the whole way around the traffic pattern because my palms were sweating so badly.

I don't remember how good my landings were, but I successfully made three of them in a row and then taxied back to where Jeff was waiting. Talk about a memorable moment! That solo flight and those stalls that Jeff taught me during the first lesson are still crystal clear in my mind almost forty years later.

On August 4, 1976, exactly six months after that first flight lesson, I passed my exams and became a private pilot—by far, the most exciting adventure of my short life. I turned twenty eleven days after obtaining my license, and I graduated from college just four months later, in December. Life was busy and it was good, and although I now knew just about everything—remember, I was twenty—my newly acquired ability to fly would continue to teach me valuable lessons for a long time to come.

Two

My Flying History

WHAT MAKES AN AIRPLANE FLY? WELL, IF YOU REMEMBER SOME of the things you read in the first chapter, you might answer, "the Bernoulli principle." But you'd be wrong—the answer is "money." That's an old joke I've used for years, and unfortunately, it has way too much truth in it. Lack of funds and the time constraints of graduate school (graduated 1978), my first "real" job (started 1978), marriage (1980), the birth of our first son (1981), and the birth of our second son (1982) didn't allow for much flying. The FAA requires private pilots to complete a biennial flight review, and if the pilots want to carry passengers they must have executed three takeoffs and landings in the previous ninety days. That's not much flying, and sadly, I was so busy that I did little more than those bare minimums.

I received my license in August 1976, and for the remainder of that year I only flew two more times with Jeff. He helped me get checked out in a Cessna 172 because I wanted the ability to rent this ubiquitous old standby—I also wanted to fly a high-wing plane just to see what it was like. All told I flew a total of 5.5 hours on five separate flights from August 1976 to November 1976.

In 1977, I flew a measly 8.2 hours for the entire year. I flew almost every month, but some of the flights lasted only around thirty minutes. Half of the year I was still in Lynchburg and my flying was done in a Cessna 172, but for the second half of that year I was living back in Pennsylvania. It was there, at the Altoona–Blair County Airport, that I was approved to rent both a Piper 151 and a Piper 140—I still preferred these low-wing planes to the high-wing Cessnas.

The best flight of 1977 was in October, when I rented a Piper 151 and took my grandfather, my father, and my brother Dan up for an hour over the Altoona area, where all four of us were born. The winds were kind as we flew above family homes and several other familiar sites. My brother told me after we landed that the only time he was "concerned" was when we were coming down on final approach. There was an old barn in line with the flight path that kept growing larger as the ground came closer, and for a minute or two he was afraid we might hit it.

My most memorable flying adventure in 1978 was performing a required biennial flight review. I had flown just 2.7 hours all year long until the end of October, but after flying one hour with an instructor on November 2, I was able to fly for another hour on November 5 and pass the review. I still enjoyed the thrill of flying, but with only 4.7 hours of flying time for the entire year, I knew I was at the bare minimum of proficiency; the handwriting was on the wall.

June 7, 1979, ended up being the last day I would fly as a pilot in command for over twenty-five years. It was a Thursday, one year to the day before our wedding, and Gail and I, along with another couple, prepared to take a short sightseeing trip. At this time I was back in Virginia, working at my first real job after graduate school. I had liked Virginia while attending college there, so when the opportunity came to move back, I jumped at the chance. We rented a Cessna 172 from Lynchburg Regional Airport for a quick hop to nearby Smith Mountain Lake—about twenty minutes away.

We had a nice calm flight to the lake and back, but between the uneventful takeoff and landing in Lynchburg, there was a landing at the lake that wasn't the best. For some reason we decided to land at Smith Mountain Lake airport. This is a much smaller airport than the ones I was accustomed to, and it also has an unusual feature—the large man-made lake off one end of the runway. (Readers who are pilots already know where this story is going.) When flying over water on final approach for a landing, depth perception is distorted and it's more difficult to determine the plane's height above the ground—especially if you've never done it before and you're at an unfamiliar airport. I came in high, and even though the runway was 3,000 feet in length, I landed long and stopped just beyond the end of the runway. Fortunately the ground was flat and our speed was slow, so only my pride was hurt. My passengers were fine and not nearly as upset about the landing as I was. We all got out, stretched, looked around a bit, checked the plane, and then loaded up for the flight back.

"All's well that ends well," as the saying goes, but I knew I couldn't continue to fly so infrequently and still maintain an acceptable level of safety. Reluctantly, I had to assent to what I knew was best—grounding myself until I could afford to fly more often. Unfortunately, the hiatus would prove to be a long one.

It was just a little over eight years later, in August 1987, that I finally got to fly again in a small plane—a Cessna 150, with John Heath as the instructor. John was working for Liberty University and trying hard to establish the school's fledgling aviation program. The plane was owned by the school, and John wanted to use the plane to make a short video that could be used for promoting the program. I was working for the university too, and this project—although outside the usual parameters of my job—sounded exciting. Family, job, building a house, and building a small business on the side had been consuming every waking hour, and I hadn't had time to even think about flying in quite awhile.

On a Wednesday, John and I, along with Dave Locke (another CFI at Liberty), met at the airport where we had access to both of the school's C-150s. It was a typical hot, humid summer day as we took off from Lynchburg Regional with John and me in one plane and Dave in the other. We went up and shot video for over half an hour of Dave in his C-150, and then both planes landed at a small airport called Brookneal. This little strip had no tower and wasn't being used that day, so we were able to get some nice takeoff and landing footage, including some great shots with the sun setting in the background. Flying was everything I remembered, and I even got to do a fair amount of it myself when I wasn't operating the camera—as they say, "just like riding a bike."

Little did I know at the time of making the video that for the next seventeen years I would only be flying in the big silver tubes rather than the small planes I enjoyed so much.

—

In 2000 I purchased a sixty-acre tract of land in Bedford County, Virginia, near Lynchburg, that had some of the best mountain views in the area. The property was mostly wooded with some open fields at the front, and my intention was to develop the land and build houses. It took a few years to cut down some of the trees, construct the roads, and install the electric lines, water lines, and so on, but by 2005 the first houses were being built. I thought it would be helpful for marketing to have aerial photo documentation of the project; it would also be a business expense and a good reason to fly again!

I forget how I first met Anthony Bickles, but he was working as a CFI for Liberty while finishing up his college degree. He was a nice young man and a good instructor. I introduced myself, told him I wanted to do a photo flight, and that I also had my pilot's license. What a great way to mix business and pleasure—I got to fly left seat to the photo site, take pictures, fly back, and even fly the pattern as we set up to land.

We flew together two times in 2005 and two more times in 2006. Each time, I got some great pictures, and was surprised once again at how quickly I felt comfortable flying. Anthony also provided two additional services: He introduced me to Ernie Rogers, a genuinely likeable guy who was instrumental in building Liberty's aviation program, and he allowed my sons to go along when we flew. By this time, both CJ and Nathan were either out of college or close to graduation, and these flights made me wish we could have enjoyed flying together when they were younger. All too quickly, Anthony graduated and left the area, so in 2007 and 2008 I had to find other instructors.

I used three different CFIs during 2007 and 2008 and went up to take pictures three more times. By now CJ was living in Philadelphia and Nathan was living in Blacksburg, Virginia, so neither of them was available to fly with me. However, my parents were visiting during two of those three photo flights, and my dad had a great time going up on both occasions. After the photo part of the flight, we would spend some time doing slow flight, steep turns, and other practice maneuvers, and Dad only asked to get out of the plane once! What a trouper, and truthfully, I scheduled those photo flights because I knew he was coming to visit.

CJ and Nathan after a photo flight.

My next big flying adventure wouldn't begin until the end of January 2013, but the seeds that would produce the fruit of that upcoming exploit had already been planted. In November 2002 Gail and I were browsing for some Christmas presents in our local Barnes & Noble. After finding the books we wanted, we bought some coffee and went to a table near the magazine racks. While waiting for my coffee to cool, I walked over to the magazines and spotted a small section I hadn't noticed before—flying! Hmm, how had I missed that? There weren't many choices. One was *Flying Magazine,* another was *AOPA Pilot,* and then there was one I had never seen before called *Kitplanes.* I picked it up, took it back to our table, opened it, and couldn't believe what I was reading. People were actually building their own planes! And these weren't just hang gliders or ultra-lights—these were actual planes. All kinds of planes: high wing, low wing, aluminum, tube and fabric, carbon fiber, plastic, two-seaters, four-seaters, one-seaters, and more. I didn't even know that it was legal to build a plane, and yet here on these pages were some extraordinarily beautiful flying machines.

"Fools rush in where angels fear to tread" and "ignorance is bliss" come to mind when I think back on that moment. But—in my defense—I did like to work with my hands, and big projects didn't scare me. I was a homebuilder who had completed a few structures that would probably be considered outside the norm. So even though I had never built a plane before, I was capable of reading blueprints and plans and believed I had the resources, stamina and determination to complete this type of venture. I might not have had the experience and specific knowledge that would have been helpful, but I figured that could be obtained one step at a time. Wheels were turning in my head, and as we sat there finishing our coffee, I was already planning how I could rearrange my shop to accommodate a lot of plane parts.

Three

Experimental Aviation

THE HISTORY OF AMATEUR-BUILT AIRCRAFT, OR HOMEBUILDING, and the history of powered flight itself are so intertwined that they really can't be separated. Even if Wilbur and Orville Wright and Samuel Pierpont Langley had commercial objectives in mind, their first manned planes were still constructed because they were passionate enthusiasts whose main goal was to fly. The race to this objective was intensely pursued by a persistent handful of intrepid homebuilders from other countries also—men like Germany's Karl Jatho, New Zealand's Richard William Pearse, Austria's Wilhelm Kress, Bavaria's Gustav Weisskopf, England's Sir Hiram Maxim, Russia's Alexander Mozhaysky, and France's Clement Ader. All of these adventurers may have been seeking fame and fortune, but they had another driving passion too—they wanted to soar like the birds.

Competition was fierce for first-flight honors, but most historians agree that the modern age of powered flight began December 17, 1903. That was the day Orville Wright made the first sustained powered flight, staying aloft for twelve seconds in a plane he and his brother Wilbur had built. This first flight may have only lasted twelve seconds, but it was the spark that caused a worldwide bonfire. The Wrights' second plane, dubbed Flyer II, flew well over one hundred times in 1904, with the longest flight an impressive five minutes in duration. In October 1905, Flyer III was given a 25-HP engine and flew for an amazing thirty-eight minutes. No one else at that time was even close to such an accomplishment, and all other would-be pilots were only able to sustain flight for a few seconds.

It was at this very pinnacle of their success that the Wrights stopped flying and began to focus instead on the business side of their venture. They didn't fly in 1906 or 1907; however, they were working on a new plane in 1907. Their new plane, the Model A two-seater, was first flown in 1908 and then passed the U.S. Army's official test of endurance—a one-hour flight—in 1909. At about that same time, the Wrights contracted with the Short Brothers, a manufacturing firm in England, to construct six flying machines. These became the first airplanes built on a production line anywhere in the world. The brothers from Ohio were beginning to get out of their homebuilding mindset and into a business mode.

Big strides were made in those first six years of sustained, powered flight: The entire industrial world was involved in efforts to build better flying machines in the hope of exploiting this newfound science for business and military purposes. Thus, World War I (1914–1918) and the years leading up to the war saw significant improvements in flight technology. Indicative of this rapid growth is the fact that before the war, in 1912, there were already 2,490 certified pilots worldwide. France had the greatest number at 966; Great Britain had 382, Germany 345, the United States 193, Italy 186, and Russia 162. The remaining 256 pilots were registered in eleven other countries. Clearly, France was the world's hotbed of aviation activity in those early days.

After the war, the Air Mail Act of 1925 facilitated the creation of a profitable commercial airline industry in the United States, and airline companies such as Pan American Airways, Western Air Express, and Ford Air Transport Service began scheduled commercial passenger service. By the 1930s, four major domestic airlines had begun operations—United, American, Eastern, and TWA—and these names would dominate commercial travel for most of the twentieth century.

With all this activity and with the need to maintain safety in the skies, the federal government was urged by many in the aviation industry to become more involved. Eventually the Air Commerce Act was passed (in 1926), and the groundwork was laid for what we know today as the FAA. This new legislation charged the Secretary of Commerce with promoting air commerce, issuing and enforcing air traffic rules, licensing pilots, certifying aircraft, establishing airways, and operating aids to air navigation. In 1934 the Department of Commerce renamed the Aeronautics Branch the Bureau of Air Commerce to reflect the growing importance of aviation to the nation. In 1938 and 1940, President Franklin Roosevelt made a few legislative changes and formed the Civil Aeronautics Authority (CAA) and the Civil Aeronautics Board (CAB). This structure stayed in place until 1958, when President Dwight D. Eisenhower signed a bill that transferred the functions of the CAA to a new independent agency—the Federal Aviation Agency. One last major change would come in 1967, when President Lyndon Johnson made the Federal Aviation Agency a part of the Department of Transportation and renamed it the Federal Aviation Administration (FAA). At the same time, the Civil Aeronautics Board's accident investigation function was transferred to the newly formed National Transportation Safety Board (NTSB).

That, in a nutshell, is how the FAA was formed, and this brief history shows just how rapidly flying evolved in fifty or sixty short years. In fact, the entire history of sustained powered flight covers a very brief span of time, and in that limited time the advances have been extraordinary. Even the most jaded should be impressed by such leaps in progress—from first flights in 1903, to breaking the sound barrier in 1947, to landing men on the moon in 1969.

My reason for including this brief history is to illustrate how "homebuilding" or "amateur-built" or "kit planes" or "experimentals" (whatever you choose to call them) have been a part of aviation from the very beginning. Today, experimental planes are constructed by many adventurous souls for whom plane-building is not a professional activity. These aircraft are generally built from kits with engineered drawings and explicit directions, and with the advent of the internet, major kit manufacturers now have support groups and websites that provide a new builder with valuable information.

There are some enthusiasts, however, who eschew the ease and prepackaged resources that a kit provides and instead build strictly from a set of plans. This obviously requires fabrication of many individual parts and is not for the faint of heart. And just like those early pioneers who started with an idea and a clean sheet of paper, there are still a few who go one step further—those aeronautical engineering types who, wanting something unique, design and build solely from an image in their imagination.

In the June 1910 issue of *Popular Mechanics* magazine, a Brazilian aviation pioneer named Alberto Santos-Dumont was the first to offer construction plans for a plane—one that he had built and flown himself in 1908. Santos-Dumont named his plane the *Demoiselle,* and *Popular Mechanics* said, "This machine is better than any other which has ever been built, for those who wish to reach results with the least possible expense and with a minimum of experimenting." That is pretty high praise, especially for a plane that supposedly could be built in fifteen days. (That reminds me of an episode I saw on a program called *Junkyard Wars*. On this particular episode the competing teams each had to construct a functioning plane from scrap parts in two days and then fly it. Scary stuff!)

Two decades after the Wright brothers' first flight, Orland G. Corben ("Ace") thought that flying had become a rich man's luxury. He decided to design a plane that was safe, easy to fly, and inexpensive--something the average person could build and operate. He began his work in 1923, and five years later he had created and marketed the first kit-built airplane, appropriately called the "Baby Ace." This became the first popular home-built aircraft, and kits continue to be sold even today.

Another homebuilder of the same era was Bernard Pietenpol, a self-taught mechanic born in 1901. By 1923 he was designing planes, and in 1928 the design that was named after him flew for the first time. In 1933, Pietenpol constructed a factory and began creating and selling partially constructed aircraft kits. Since he lived until 1984, he was able to both contribute to, and observe, amazing advances in flight. The iconic "Pietenpol," like the Baby Ace, has withstood the test of time and is still being built today.

The 1930s also saw the creation of several amateur aircraft organizations, the outworking of worldwide excitement following Charles Lindbergh's solo transatlantic crossing in May 1927. No doubt the early concentration of pilots in France, referenced earlier, is the reason an association of amateur aviation enthusiasts was created in France in 1936 (this fact may also explain why Lindbergh chose Paris, not Dublin or London, for his transatlantic destination). Ten years later, 1946 saw the birth of the Ultralight Aircraft Association (later the Popular Flying Association) in the United Kingdom, followed in 1953 by the Sport Aircraft Association in Australia and the Experimental Aircraft Association (EAA) in the United States. The EAA is an international organization of aviation enthusiasts based in Oshkosh, Wisconsin. It was founded by Paul Poberezny, a thirty-year career Air Force pilot with over 30,000 hours of flight time. He is said to have flown over 500 different aircraft types (including over 170 home-built planes) in a lifetime of flying adventures that started at age 16 and lasted until his death at age 91—as chronicled in his autobiography, *Poberezny: The Story Begins.* I'll always treasure an EAA hat that Paul graciously signed for me in 2011.

Today the EAA, which began in the basement of the Poberezny home in Hales Corners, Wisconsin, is a world-class organization with approximately 170,000 members in over 100 countries. EAA's annual convention and fly-in, known as EAA AirVenture Oshkosh—or, more commonly, just "Oshkosh"—is an annual week-long celebration that attracts more than 500,000 people. This largest fly-in in the United States also brings in 10,000 to 12,000 planes, and for one week out of the year Wittman Regional Airport is known as the busiest airport in the world. It's no accident that it was at Oshkosh a few years ago that Burt Rutan (homebuilder extraordinaire) and Sir Richard Branson (billionaire adventurer) announced that they were forming a business, Virgin Galactic, that would carry civilian passengers into space. Sometime in the near future this fledgling company is supposed to make its maiden space flight, with Branson and two of his children on board.

Fifty years after the Wrights first flew, EAA and EAA AirVenture Oshkosh were formed to keep the spirit of homebuilding going strong and to nurture all things aeronautical. Today, although much of their work is still directed at supporting those involved in E-AB (experimental amateur-built) aircraft, they also work with ultra-lights, light sport aircraft, vintage aircraft, and warbirds.

The number of homebuilt planes in the United States keeps growing each year. In fact, the FAA says that "the amateur-built aircraft fleet has shown the most consistent growth of any aircraft category in the U.S. over the past twenty years, even during recessionary periods." They also estimate that in 2011 the total number of homebuilts was almost 33,000 and that this number represents more than fifteen percent of the entire U.S. single-engine, piston-powered fleet. That's a lot of dedicated people who've spent quite a few hours working in their backyard shop or hangar. (However, in relation to our national population of around 317 million in 2013, the numbers are still extremely small: Less than .02% of the population has ever built and registered a personal airplane.)

The magazine that almost all those intrepid homebuilding souls subscribe to and follow faithfully is *Kitplanes*—the world's foremost experimental aviation magazine. Since 1984, this monthly publication of glossy photos, detailed illustrations, meticulous narratives, life-saving safety reminders, and encouraging stories is considered by many to be the Holy Grail of experimental plane builders. The magazine claimed approximately 36,000 faithful subscribers in 2013, many of whom would probably sacrifice a meal each day before they would give up this invaluable resource.

The January 2013 issue of *Kitplanes* listed 142 planes for which plans could be purchased today—everything from some of the 1928 classics to contemporary designs that can cruise at 200 mph or more. Although the majority of people who want to build their own plane choose to do so by purchasing and assembling a kit from a reliable manufacturer, not all planes are available in kit form. Sometimes the only option is to buy a set of plans and start making the parts yourself—a daunting task by any standard. However, if you have the mechanical abilities and the time, you can save quite a bit by choosing this path to plane ownership.

But since time and talent are in limited supply for most of us, and since there is such a wide array of kits to choose from (363 in 2013), most enthusiasts opt to build from a kit. Yes, it's going to cost more, but in the long run you stand a greater chance of completing the project before you die—or quit in frustration. Let's say that you take 2,000 hours (supposedly a reasonable estimate) to build your plane. What does this translate to in years? Obviously, the answer lies in how many hours per week you can invest in the project. Working forty hours per week, you could conceivably finish in a year; working just five to ten hours on weekends will extend the project considerably. I've read that if we discard both those projects that are finished in a year, and those that go on for twenty years (oh yes, and some even longer), three to seven years is a reasonable expectation.

When choosing which plane to build, there are numerous factors to consider that go well beyond the initial decision of whether or not to build from a kit. Questions such as "How much money can I spend?", "How much time do I honestly have?", and "What style of plane do I want?" are good places to start, but you should also consider the purpose or "mission" of the plane, the completeness of the kit, and the reputation (and longevity) of the manufacturer. It's also critical to consider the support provided, the potential for resale, and the success rate of other builders. Once into the project, there will be dozens of additional decisions to be made, from the type and make of engine (and propeller) to interior finishes, exterior design, lighting, and instrument panel. Within each of those broad categories is still a wide array of additional choices.

It's been said that building an airplane isn't a big job, just a whole bunch of little ones. First and foremost the task requires perseverance, then a desire to learn, a certain mechanical aptitude, and attention to detail—a *lot* of detail. In addition, you'll need the ability to make decisions and an adequate space in which to build (although I know of one guy who did much of his work in a New York City apartment).

With all these considerations taken into account, and after a test flight at Sun 'n Fun, I decided in 2003 to undertake the construction of a Van's RV-7A airplane. Van's is the largest kit plane manufacturer in the world, and the RV-7A is a proven design with over 1,300 planes completed and flying. Although the word "experimental" would have to be displayed clearly in the cockpit of my future plane, I was not qualified to push the envelope too hard and preferred instead to construct something that had a proven reputation.

So with 100 years of history and two months of research behind me, the decision was made, and I prepared to take the first step of a very long journey.

Four

Builder's Log

HOW DO YOU BEGIN TO DESCRIBE A PROJECT THAT STARTED WITH a dream in 2003 and culminated with the first flight of an airplane, built with my own hands, in 2013—a project that for months at a time was all-consuming? It absorbed virtually all of my non-employment-related time, because when I wasn't physically working on a part, I was researching something on the computer, or doing mental gymnastics as I tried to solve a particular challenge. There were many fitful nights when I wrestled with a problem all night long. This plane inspired my dreams, but it also stole my sleep, occupied my days, manipulated my thoughts, monopolized my conversation, and generally—sometimes to my detriment—became the focus of my life. It was also one of the most enjoyable and rewarding experiences I've ever had.

The entire process was documented in a logbook I was required to keep by the FAA. This, along with a collection of pictures, is what was needed to demonstrate at the end of the project that I was indeed the builder. The FAA requires all builders of experimental airplanes to show that they have constructed at least 51 percent of the plane.

You'll notice that it did not take me ten working years to build the plane. I may have started in 2003 and flown in 2013, but there was a five-and-a-half-year interruption after the first year or so of construction. All together it took me two years and nine months of actual labor—a little over 1,800 hours—to construct the plane. Left unrecorded, however, were almost as many additional hours of research and computer time, since this was my first building experience.

I've put the ensuing text of the logbook in smaller print because it is lengthy and would be extremely tedious to read straight through from beginning to end. I encourage you to skim this chapter, taking note of the dates, the number of hours accrued, the detail involved, and the commentary I've inserted (in normal size print) when a particularly interesting part of the build is being described.

2/03	Spent most of this month taking a large stack of pine and fir timbers and cutting them into fireplace mantels. Three steps were involved: (1) Cut both ends square and to the desired length; (2) sand three sides very well and sand the back side lightly; (3) router a decorative edge on three sides, both top and bottom. Ended up with 82 mantels. Next step is to apply two coats of polyurethane to each mantel, but I'll only do about ten for now. I'll do the rest as I am selling them. This project served two purposes. First, it will free up a lot of space in the shop, and second, it should generate between five and seven thousand dollars to be used for purchasing kit materials.
3/1/03	Spent yesterday and today cleaning up the sawdust and mess from the mantel project. Also, did some rearranging in the shop to better accommodate bench and tool placement. The entire plane with wings attached will fit inside the shop.
3/5/03	Installed more shelving and built workbench in shop. Also hung a drop light from the ceiling and bolted a new vise to an old workbench. Also ordered a drill press and bench sander from Grizzly.
4/2/03	Attended Sun 'n Fun in Lakeland, FL. Flew in an RV-7A. Great!

This was the first time I'd ever been to either Sun 'n Fun or Oshkosh, and this event was a real eye-opener to the world of home-building. To this point my main exposure had been *Kitplanes* magazine. My parents went with Gail and me, and we all had a good time. Also, even though I had already decided which kit I wanted to build, flying in the company's RV-7A demonstrator definitely sealed the decision.

5/2/03	Mounted drill press and bench sander to workbench.
11/29/03	Cleaned off the shelves of all remaining pool stuff.
12/29/03	Chris Collins brought over his dump truck, and I filled it by cleaning out the shop and cleaning up stuff around the outside of the shop.
1/10/04	Mounted two sheets of 4′ × 8′ pegboard onto shop wall.
1/31/04	Purchased, assembled, and mounted to workbench a 6-inch grinder.
2/21/04	Joined EAA chapter 646 in Roanoke.
5/04	Built rollable rack for holding storage containers on one side and plane plans on the other side.
6/04	Ordered plane tools from a guy in Chicago who bought them new a year ago and built his empennage with them. He had around $2,600 invested and I bought them for $2,100.
7/27–8/2/04	Attended Oshkosh. Bought just a couple of tools. Riveted for the first time at a seminar.
8/24/04	Ordered quick-build wings and fuselage and empennage.
8/31/04	Empennage arrived by FedEx truck. Busy with wastewater treatment plant. Wings & fuselage won't be here until late December. I'll probably wait until December to attend empennage seminar in Georgia and get started. I did inventory empennage parts at this time.

This may seem like a small thing, but when those first plane parts arrive at your home, it is really exciting! I even took a picture of the woman driving the FedEx truck and then told her all about my plans. She seemed genuinely interested, and she smiled. I probably put her behind schedule.

9/1–9/20/04	Have been looking at all of the RV-7 websites every evening for a couple of hours. Several are very detailed and helpful. I am thinking about just jumping into the empennage and working on it without the benefit of the class in Georgia.
9/23/04	Worked with the new air tools for a couple of hours. Figured out how to operate and set up the pneumatic squeezer and the rivet gun.
9/25/04	Practiced squeezing rivets and bucking rivets for about 3 hours.
9/27/04	Sorted bags of small parts into jars. Labeled jars. Sorted larger parts into various empennage sections. 4 hrs.
9/28/04	Started working on the horizontal stabilizer (HS). 2 hrs.

So after over a year and a half of planning, getting the shop organized, and learning how to use tools that I had never even seen before, I was actually putting together a part of a plane—a machine that would someday enable me to soar through the sky. To say this was thrilling is a terrible, terrible understatement.

9/29/04	Horizontal stabilizer. 4hrs.
9/30/04	Horizontal stabilizer. Cut 2 ribs incorrectly while trying to work and watch the presidential debates at the same time. 4 hrs.
10/1/04	Horizontal stabilizer. 2 hrs.
10/2/04	Vertical stabilizer (VS). Switched to vertical stabilizer while waiting for the replacement parts needed for the horizontal stabilizer. Assemble and drill. 3 hrs.
10/3/04	Vertical stabilizer. Deburr and dimple. 5 hrs.
10/4/04	Vertical stabilizer. Rivet rear spar. 3 hrs.
10/5/04	Vertical stabilizer. Start riveting skin to ribs and front spar. 2.5 hrs.
10/6/04	Vertical stabilizer is done. Received the two HS 404 ribs today that I cut incorrectly, so it's back to the horizontal stabilizer tomorrow. 5 hrs.
10/7/04	Horizontal stabilizer. Assembled and drilled. 9 hrs.
10/8/04	Horizontal stabilizer. Deburred. 3.5 hrs.
10/11/04	Horizontal stabilizer. Dimpled. 3 hrs. Went to PA this past weekend for my Grandmother Focht's 90th birthday. Thus no plane work done on the 9th and 10th.
10/12/04	Horizontal stabilizer. Sanded, primed, and started riveting. 6.5 hrs.
10/13/04	Horizontal stabilizer. Riveting is difficult by yourself. 6 hrs.
10/14/04	Horizontal stabilizer. Riveting went easier tonight. 3 hrs.
10/15/04	Horizontal stabilizer. Finished riveting. Did not put the rear spar in place because tomorrow I am going to take the HS and the VS to our EAA chapter meeting so that I can be criticized to death. Our technical advisor will be at the meeting. Started to highlight the rudder plans and check out a couple of websites for rudder information. 4 hrs.
10/16/04	Horizontal stabilizer. Took my HS with me and met with Bob Barrows, our local EAA technical advisor, at his airport in Fincastle. He pointed out a few needed adjustments on my HS. Overall [it] was good, but there is always room for improvement. Came home later in the day and worked on making those improvements. 2 hrs.

We are fortunate to have Bob Barrows, designer of the well-known Bearhawk line of kit planes, in our local EAA chapter. Bob was gracious enough to offer his time as a technical counselor. The FAA recommends having a technical counselor inspect your plane several times over the course of the project, and I was glad to have Bob look things over on two separate occasions.

10/17/04	Horizontal stabilizer. Paul Reeves came over this Sunday afternoon and helped me finish the HS by riveting on the rear spar. 3 hrs.
10/18/04	Rudder. Cut the stiffeners, then assembled and drilled stiffeners. 5.5 hrs.
10/19/04	Rudder. Cut plastic coating on skins and deburred. 2 hrs.
10/20/04	Rudder. Back-riveted stiffeners. 2 hrs.
10/21/04	Rudder. Assembled and drilled. 3 hrs.
10/22/04	Rudder. Deburred, dimpled, sanded, and primed. 7.5 hrs.
10/23/04	Rudder. Finished dimpling and started riveting. 8 hrs.
10/24/04	Rudder. More riveting and formed the trailing edge. 4.5 hrs.
10/25/04	Rudder. Riveted trailing edge and rolled leading edge. Finished rudder. 5 hrs.
	109 hrs. total to this point.

10/26/04	Right elevator. Marked the plans and started assembly. 2.5 hrs.
10/28/04	Right elevator. Assembled, drilled, and cut stiffeners. 4 hrs.
10/30/04	Right elevator. Finished and back-riveted stiffeners. Mom and Dad were visiting this weekend. Dad helped. He deburred and dimpled the stiffeners. 4 hrs.
10/31/04	Right elevator. Prepared the skeleton and started riveting. 7 hrs.
11/1/04	Right elevator. Finished riveting. Finished right elevator. 6 hrs.
11/2/04	Left elevator. Marked the plans. Cut and smoothed stiffeners. 3 hrs.
11/3/04	Left elevator. Assembled, drilled, deburred, and dimpled stiffeners and skin. Discovered that I had cut 6 of the stiffeners incorrectly. I'll have to order new stiffener material tomorrow. 2.5 hrs.
11/4/04	Left elevator. Riveted stiffeners and put plate nuts on access door. 1.5 hrs.
11/6/04	Left elevator. Back-riveted access door to skin; assembled, drilled, and deburred everything except the skin. 5 hrs.
11/7/04	Left elevator. Deburred and smoothed edges of skin. Dimpled skeleton and riveted most of skeleton. 5.5 hrs.

11/9/04	Left elevator. Remade the six stiffeners that I cut too short the first time. 2 hrs.
11/14/04	Left elevator. Deburred and dimpled skin, then back-riveted the six stiffeners. Paul Reeves came over to help for a couple of hours. Started to work on installing the elevator trim electric motor. 4.5 hrs.
11/24/04	Left elevator. Messed up the mount for the trim motor. Will need to order a new part next week. Bent the inside flanges for the elevator. 2 hrs.

I believe this is the third part that I messed up. Get used to it. It happens.

11/28/04	Left elevator. The inside flange bends worked well. Dimpled the remaining holes and started to rivet. 3 hrs.
11/30/04	Left elevator. Did some more riveting. 1.5 hrs.
12/2/04	Left elevator. Worked on mounting trim motor to cover skin. 2.5 hrs.
12/4/04	Left elevator. Bent edges for trim-tab skin and installed trim motor. 5.5 hrs.
12/5/04	Left elevator. Finished riveting and installed hinge for trim tab. 7 hrs.
12/6/04	Left elevator. Rolled, drilled, and blind-riveted edges for both left and right elevator. 5.5 hrs.
12/7/04	Elevators. Installed rod end bearings. Used vise grips with a cushion between the teeth, then saw a homemade tool on Jim Smith's website. Hung the elevators on the HS. Looks great. 4 hrs.
12/8/04	Elevators. Fine-tuned elevators to make them both even off of the trailing edge of the stabilizer. 2 hrs.
12/9/04	Elevators. Called Van's to find out if it is OK if the elevator horns don't both hang at the same angle. 1 hr.
12/10/04	Elevators. Drilled hole through main middle bushing into each elevator. 2 hrs.

170 hrs. total to this point.

Me in the shop.

12/21/04	Empennage has been done (except for the fiberglass tips) for a couple of weeks now. I am anxiously awaiting the quick-build wings and fuselage. I rearranged the shop yesterday and today to better accommodate the large parts. 3 hrs.
12/30/04	Nathan helped me build a front and rear support piece for the fuselage. We covered the pieces with old wet suits for padding. 3 hrs.
1/4/05	Quick-build wings and fuselage were boxed and shipped out from Van's today. I've been looking closely for the last 3 weeks at 2 or 3 websites of builders who have gone the quick-build route.
1/8/05	Started working on the empennage tip fairings. They got bent out of shape when shipped, so I used a heat gun, some wooden shims for wedges, and a bucket of cold water to get them in shape. 6 hrs.
1/9/05	Continued working on tip fairings. 6 hrs.
1/10/05	Still working on tip fairings. 1 hr.
1/13/05	Borrowed truck and trailer from Chris Collins and went to Roanoke to pick up 2 boxes that contained my QB wings and fuselage. Loading went smoothly, and unloading was a piece of cake. Used my tractor and Winnie Yeats's forks. Had to modify the forks and make them 4′ 6″ long; they are only 3′ 3″ long normally. Pried the top off of the fuselage box. Pretty neat. I'll start inventorying tomorrow. 6 hrs.

Some kit manufacturers will partially assemble the fuselage or the wings—for an additional fee, of course. This is allowable as long as you are still doing 51 percent of the building yourself. For me, this was an acceptable additional amount of money to spend in order to keep the building experience within a reasonable time frame—one best suited to my goals. I didn't want the project to go on for six or eight years; I wanted to be flying in about three years.

1/14/05	Disassembled the big box (4′ × 4′ × 16′) and started to unwrap [parts] and [do] inventory. They use a lot of paper, and this thing is very well packed. Put the fuselage up on the sawhorses. 5 hrs.
1/15/05	Continued to inventory and put small items into jars. 6 hrs.
1/16/05	Finished inventory by laying out parts on the shelves and built holding jig for wings. Uncrated wings and placed them in their jig. 6 hrs.

1/17/05	The weather has turned bitterly cold (five below zero) almost overnight. Spent a couple hours in the shop comparing fuselage plans to the actual fuselage. 2 hrs.
1/18–1/20/05	Spending this week looking at websites and looking over each of the plan sheets. 6 hrs.
1/22/05	Removed various floor and rear baggage panels from fuselage, installed firewall recessed panel, and started on installing steps. 10 hrs.
1/23/05	Installed, drilled, deburred, and dimpled top aft fuselage skin. 6 hrs.
1/24/05	Removed aft fuselage skin and worked on steps. 5 hrs.
1/25/05	Drilled, shaped, sanded, and primed steps. 2 hrs.
1/26/05	Removed broken fuselage rib and installed right step; deburred, dimpled, and edge-sanded fuselage skin. 4 hrs.
1/27/05	Sorted out rudder and brake pedal assembly. 2 hrs.
1/28/05	Installed right side step. Started working on rudder and brake pedal assembly. 3 hrs.
1/29/05	Finished rudder and brake pedal except for drilling plastic blocks to longerons. I put the firewall recess in too soon and may have to remove it. Started working on seat backs. 10 hrs.
1/30/05	Continued working on seat backs. I need another 16″ of piano hinge if I intend to install the hinged seat back supports. I may not install these because it makes a neater interior finish if I don't. 8 hrs.
1/31/05	Riveted second seat back. Drilled & cut rudder pedal blocks and then mounted rudder pedals. Made holes for two different locations. 4 hrs.
2/1/05	Finished rudder pedal brace and worked on seat back hinge supports. 4 hrs.
2/2/05	Finished seat back hinge supports and started on landing gear weldment. Hard to get bolts installed. 6.5 hrs.
2/3/05	Finished both landing gear weldments. Had to take the first one back out after I had gotten all the bolts in because I forgot to pre-drill the landing gear leg. 4 hrs.
2/4/05	Started assembly of roll bar. 6 hrs.
2/5/05	Finished roll bar and had Nathan help me rivet brake hose bracket onto firewall. 12 hrs.
2/6/05	Started attaching roll bar to fuselage. 3 hrs.
2/7/05	Still attaching roll bar to fuselage. This is tricky. 2 hrs.
2/8/05	Continuing to attach roll bar to fuselage. The hard part of adjusting, grinding, and adjusting again is done. Temperature reached 68° today. 3 hrs.
2/9/05	Finished attaching roll bar to fuselage. 3 hrs.

2/10/05	Finished roll bar and started putting in replacement baggage area rib that I broke last month. 2 hrs.
2/12/05	Paul Reeves helped me rivet in the baggage area rib. Then I finished attaching the left side step. Also finished dimpling the top skin that I thought I had dimpled on 1/23/05. And I drilled the four #10 holes on the inside of the roll bar. 6 hrs.
2/13/05	Looked over the plans for awhile, deciding on my next step. Started to install the horizontal stabilizer. Highlighted the plans. 6 hrs.
2/14/05	Installed horizontal stabilizer and started to install vertical stabilizer. 4 hrs.
2/15/05	Attached elevators and determined which [horn] was the aft horn. Drilled a hole in the aft horn and then made a drill guide from ¾″ aluminum with which to drill the hole in the other horn. Then installed vertical stabilizer. 4 hrs.
2/16/05	Finished the vertical stabilizer. This included riveting the aft stop and making and riveting the tie-down plate. Then removed VS and HS and drilled the hole in the second elevator horn. 5 hrs.
2/17/05	Fabricated rudder stops and then riveted all rear bulkhead rivets. 3.5 hrs.
2/20/05	Took Dorothy and Gail to Greenville, SC, to see Roy and Betty. No plane work done on the 18th & 19th. Fitted rudder to VS and adjusted hinge bearings. Fits great. Drilled out rudder stops though because they were too small and allowed the rudder to hit the elevators. Will have to redo them tomorrow. 2 hrs.
2/21/05	Redid the rudder stops. What a pain. Started on front covers. 8 hrs.
2/22/05	Finished front covers. 6 hrs.
2/23/05	Finished baggage compartment floor and started looking at plans and laying out parts for electric flap installation. 7 hrs.
2/24/05	Worked on electric flap weldment. 3 hrs.
2/25/05	Worked on electric flap housing. 2 hrs.
2/26/05	Just about finished with electric flap weldment, housing, and motor. 8 hrs.
2/27/05	Flap actuator motor does not drive the internal shaft. I'll have to call Van's tomorrow and see if it is defective. Built and installed elevator bell crank. Finished up some things on the electric flap housing and started to build the tube that goes from the bell crank to the elevators. 5 hrs.
2/28/05	Finished long elevator tube and installed it. Flap motor works fine; I was just not operating it properly. Finished installation of flap actuator motor. 5 hrs

Nate helping in the shop.

You'll notice if you look closely at both the preceding and the upcoming months that I was working on the plane almost every day—usually investing eight to ten hours per day on the weekends. This is one of the keys to completing a long-term venture like this. My goal was to do something on the plane each day, even if it was just something small. Getting in the habit and staying in it is critical. Think of all those clichés you've heard during your life about "a journey of a thousand miles..." and "how do you eat an elephant?" and rest assured that they are absolutely true. I could never focus on building an airplane; instead, I had to focus on just building a single piece. The fun time, the encouraging time, comes when those smaller pieces are put together and actually start to look like a plane.

3/1/05	Marked plans for work on forward fuselage. 2 hrs.
3/2/05	Made several small parts needed for forward fuselage. 2 hrs.
3/3/05	Finished right seat back by installing piano hinge to seat back support and then made another small part for the forward fuselage. 2 hrs.
3/4/05	Made and fitted angle seal for instrument panel. Also started to assemble forward fuselage parts. 4 hrs.
3/5/05	Drilled, deburred, and did some dimpling on forward fuselage. Also riveted angle seal onto subassembly 678. 4 hrs.
3/6/05	Riveted angle seal onto instrument panel and angle seal to one curved forward fuselage subassembly. 4 hrs.

3/7/05	Repaired angle seal and then riveted it onto the other curved forward fuselage subassembly. Then prepped and primed all three main pieces in the forward fuselage subassembly. 3 hrs.
3/8/05	Assembled and clecoed forward fuselage subassembly, and then fitted and clecoed it to the fuselage. Drilled skin to subassembly. 4 hrs.
3/9/05	Fitted small brace pieces to panel. 2 hrs.
3/12/05	Nathan helped by deburring and dimpling front skin. I worked on fitting air vent under panel. 5 hrs.
3/13/05	Primed forward fuselage subassembly and installed side plastic air inlet vents. 3 hrs.
3/14/05	Drilled & mounted brake reservoir. 1 hr.
3/15/05	Stared at the plumbing plans for about an hour. Starting to figure them out. Drilled hole in bottom of fuselage for vent. 1.5 hrs.
3/16/05	Painted the forward fuselage subassembly. Cut pieces for the wing tank brace that attaches to the fuselage. Finally drilled the side hole for the fuel vent and still drilled it too close to the vertical brace. It may work though. 3 hrs.
3/17/05	Gail sang "Danny Boy" at Charley's restaurant tonight (St. Patrick's Day).
3/18/05	Fuel vent side hole did not work, so I drilled it again. Finished the wing tank brace that attaches to fuselage. 3 hrs.
3/19/05	Attached small brackets that secure panel and air vent. Dimpled firewall. Riveted half of fuselage subassembly. Started working on left vent line. 4 hrs.
3/20/05	Finished vent lines. 2 hrs.
3/22/05	Started working on fuel lines. 2 hrs.
3/23/05	Finished fuel lines from selector valve to wings. Snapped plastic bushings in ⅝" holes throughout fuselage. 2 hrs.
3/24/05	Inventoried back-ordered bag of bolts that was received today. Studied ELT installation manual. Installed rudder cable and 2 fuel-attach brackets. 2 hrs.
	455.5 hrs total to this point.
3/26/05	Studied plans and looked at websites for installing wings. Drilled out rivets in wing that should not have been installed. Tightened bolts that attach fuel tanks to wing. Installed rudder cable fairlets at rear fuselage. Nathan helped. 7 hrs.
3/27/05	Happy Easter. Fabricated and installed left and right brake lines. 4 hrs.

Yes, I even worked on Easter Sunday! But I did go to church that morning, and we had a very nice dinner just as we always do. What did I say about doing something every day?

3/28/05	Shaped rear wing attach brackets to proper size. Built dolly to place wings on when it's time to attach wings to fuselage. Made drift pins for wing attachment. 3 hrs.
3/29/05	Made short elevator pushrod and control rod. Started assembling powder-coated control parts. 3 hrs.
3/31/05	Started to install control stick parts. Put adel clamp on rudder cable tubing. Put bottom bolt in fuel tank support bracket. Bolted on shoulder harness cables. 2 hrs.
4/1/05	Started to put screens on bottom of fuel vent fittings. Installed front elevator control tube. What a pain. 2 hrs.
4/2/05	Finished screens on fuel vent fittings. Worked more on control stick parts. Installed vent tubing. Put fuel lube on brake line fittings. 4 hrs.
4/3/05	Finished control stick. Measured for braided metal brake hoses. 2 hrs.
4/9/05	Been working on Cedar Rock subdivision for the last few days. Installed aileron bellcrank; built and primed stick and aileron pushrods. 5 hrs.
4/10/05	Painted stick and aileron pushrods. Started assembling aileron brackets. 3 hrs.
4/11/05	Drilled and deburred aileron brackets. 1 hr.
4/12/05	Riveted and installed aileron brackets. 3 hrs.
4/14/05	Set wastewater treatment plant at Cedar Rock.
4/16/05	Installed attachment brackets on ailerons. 2 hrs.
4/19/05	Assembled, drilled, disassembled, deburred, and smoothed edges of left and right aileron gap fairings. 2 hrs.
4/21/05	Riveted aileron gap fairings. 1 hr.
4/22/05	Installed left aileron and studied Checkoway's website to figure out how to get it in the neutral position. 2 hrs.
4/23/05	Assembled flap braces and drilled holes to spar. Attached left aileron pushrod to aileron. Riveted left flap brace. 2 hrs.
4/24/05	Used tool provided in kit to locate aileron in neutral position; then lined up left flap. Drilled, deburred, dimpled, and riveted left wing skin, flap brace, and flap hinge. 5 hrs.
4/25/05	Installed right aileron and attached aileron pushrod. Riveted right flap brace. 2 hrs.

4/26/05	Located right aileron in neutral position; then lined up right flap. Drilled, deburred, dimpled, and riveted right wing skin, flap brace, and flap hinge. 2 hrs.
5/17/05	EAA chapter meeting at my shop from 6:00 p.m. till 8:00 p.m. Twelve guys attended. Had a good and informative time. Work on Cedar Rock has been very busy this past month. Not much plane work getting done.
5/26/05	Picked up finish kit from ABF Trucking in Roanoke. 3 hrs.
5/30/05	Uncrated finish kit and started doing inventory. 3 hrs.
5/31/05	Continued doing inventory. 2 hrs.
6/1/05	Still doing inventory. 2 hrs.
6/2/05	Finished inventory. 3 hrs.
6/3– 6/5/05	Attended aeroelectric seminar by Bob Nuckolls in NC.
6/6/05	Installed ½″ plastic conduit for wire runs to tail. 1 hr.
7/26–7/31/05	Attended Oshkosh.
10/1/05	Attended VA EAA fly-in at Petersburg. Mom & Dad went also.

526.5 hrs. total to this point.

12/21/10 My wonderful project has been sitting under wraps in the shop for the past five and a half years. I can't believe it's been that long. The Cedar Rock subdivision became very busy as we finished up the installation of the wastewater treatment plant, installed the underground utilities, and finished meeting the state specs for the construction of the roads in the second half of 2005. Then in March 2006 I started building a fairly large spec house in Cedar Rock. Over the past five and a half years, I have built and sold three large spec homes in Cedar Rock; finished off the basement of Nathan and Alex's home in the Wyndhurst area; and gutted and renovated CJ's home on Adams Drive. I purchased a new commercial building in Wyndhurst and finished off the 2nd floor for CJ's new office, helped CJ start The Lynchburg Insurance Group, helped Nathan develop BecoBall, oversaw the operation of the wastewater treatment plant in Cedar Rock—*and* performed my daily duties in the home inspection business. It's been very busy, but now BecoBall has moved out of the shop and over into the Wyndhurst office, and CJ has most of his stuff moved out of the shop into his new house.

In the last month I have repositioned and reorganized the tools and plane parts in the shop. I've also been reacquainting myself with the plane's instructions and drawings and looking at a few of the websites that have been so thoroughly documented. I'll also have to bring myself back up to speed on the use of the specialty tools. You don't do much riveting when building houses.

Being self-employed in a few real-estate-related businesses, I am often reminded that the old adage "make hay while the sun shines" doesn't just pertain to farmers. During the boom years of building—from roughly 2003 to 2008—we were working a lot of hours, and life was extremely busy (as the 12/21/10 logbook entry shows). Also, in 2008 both of my sons came back home to pursue their professional goals, having finished school, grad school, and jobs in other parts of the country. In addition, my mother-in-law needed some assistance around that time, and in 2008 she came to live with us. There was just too much going on, and the plane ended up on the back burner. Actually, it was relegated to a corner of the shop and covered with a tarp. My wife would sometimes ask when I thought I would be able to get back to work on it, and my response was, "It's not going anywhere, it's paid for, and it'll be there when I'm able."

The building bubble finally burst in 2008, and the residential housing market slowed down in our area quicker than drivers on a NASCAR track with six wrecks. We still had several loose ends to tie up, but sometime in 2010 I was able (and anxious) to get back to the plane. It took awhile to reacquaint myself with where I was and what I had already done, to study the instructions again, and to relearn how to use a couple of tools. But in a few weeks I was pretty much back up to speed.

1/17/11	Rewrote the parts numbers which had faded on several parts jars. Installed the bottom fiberglass fairing on the rudder. 4 hrs.
1/18/11	Finished the bottom fiberglass fairing on the rudder. Installed the top fiberglass fairing on the vertical stabilizer. Pulled the horizontal stabilizer and elevators off the shelf and set them up on a workbench. Looked at fitting the fairings on all of this. Drilled out ten flush rivets on the horizontal stabilizer that I should not have put in five years ago. 6 hrs.
1/19/11	Cut foam for horizontal stabilizer fiberglass fairings and installed these fiberglass fairings. 1 hr.
1/20/11	Mixed epoxy and coated the vertical and horizontal stabilizer fairings. Installed bolt and washers in the control arm/front pushrod assembly for the elevators (this bolt took almost two hours). 4 hrs.
1/21/11	Added second coat of epoxy to stabilizer fairings. Inserted wire conduit through the main spar. Installed front part of the rear

	pushrod for the elevators onto the bellcrank. Stripped the blue vinyl off the last piece of fuselage skin. 3 hrs.
1/22/11	Put pieces of the roll bar and baggage area frame together so that the final fuselage skin can be installed. Finished the edge of the final fuselage skin. 6 hrs.
1/23/11	Sanded & primed fuselage skin. Put final coat of epoxy on vertical and horizontal stabilizer fairings. 2 hrs.
1/24/11	Put finish paint on interior of fuselage skin because part of this skin will be seen in the baggage compartment. Mounted horizontal stabilizer on the fuselage. Double-checked all measurements from five years ago and then fastened it in place. 3 hrs.
1/25/11	Temporarily mounted vertical stabilizer on the fuselage. Double-checked all previous measurements. Everything was right on. Spent all day figuring out how to install the top fiberglass fairing and the bottom metal fairing. Got the bottom fairing temporarily on and got the nut plates mostly installed for the top fairing. 8 hrs.
1/27/11	Got the nutplates installed for these fairings. Drilled & fitted top fiberglass fairing and then realized that the entire edge of the fairing needs to be trimmed back. Taped off and sanded top rail of fuselage that needs to be painted. 8 hrs.
1/28/11	Painted top rail of fuselage. Trimmed edges of the empennage fiberglass fairing and believe that the fit is pretty good. 6 hrs.
1/29/11	Made a mounting bracket for the ELT. Installed this bracket along with the ELT holder and the ELT antennae; secured the ELT antennae wire to the fuselage. Painted the cabin roll bar and the top brace that secures the roll bar. Removed the elevators from the horizontal stabilizer in order to polish them more easily. Removed the horizontal stabilizer from the fuselage in order to polish it more easily. 6 hrs.
1/30/11	Installed fuselage roll bar cross brace and the roll bar. Clecoed on the top fore fuselage skin. 1 hr.
1/31/11	Tapped the 6/32" holes for aft bottom vertical stabilizer fairing. Ordered polishing equipment and polish today from PerfectPolish.com. Met Bradley Blanks and Bob Howell. These guys head up Liberty University's Aviation A&P program. Finished putting bolts into the roll bar. 5 hrs.
2/1/11	Hooked up the trim motor and the brackets that hold the trim motor. Started to reacquaint myself with the wing plans. 3 hrs.
2/3/11	CJ had major eye surgery yesterday, and it seems to have gone very well. Made the small spacers that are used for the aileron brackets and got all of the washers, nuts, and bolts ready. Hooked up both pushrods on both of the wing bellcranks. Installed six pulled rivets in the wing flap braces. Dug out both of the wing skins and got the right

	skin clecoed onto the wing. Removed the ailerons that were temporarily installed. 4 hrs.
2/4/11	Clecoed the left skin onto the left wing. Drilled both skins. Deburred both skins and dimpled the left skin. 4 hrs.
2/5/11	Dimpled the right skin and all of the ribs and braces on both wings. Worked the outer edges of both skins. Primed the inside of both skins. Nathan and Alex came to visit. Nathan dimpled several ribs and Alex dimpled one rib. 6 hrs.
2/6/11	Installed the plate nuts on both wing skin access openings. Drilled, deburred, dimpled, and finished the edges of both access covers. 2 hrs.
2/7/11	Dusted off the front top fuselage parts that were built five years ago and installed them along with the instrument panel. Fabricated and installed the hat channel. 5 hrs.
2/9/11	Received the Cyclo polisher and supplies on 2/7/11. Familiarized myself with the equipment and polished the underside of the horizontal stabilizer. 5 hrs.
2/10/11	Polished the top side of the HS and the aft fuselage area. 4 hrs.
2/11/11	Polished the right elevator. 2 hrs.
2/12/11	Polished the left elevator, trim tab, and vertical stabilizer. 6 hrs.
2/13/11	[My mother-in-law,] Dorothy, died this Sunday morning at 7:30 a.m.

At first I had considered taking several very private notations out of this diary (see 2/3/11 and 2/13/11) but I eventually decided against it. Why? Because this is just how personal a task of this magnitude can become. I thought about the plane every day and worked on it most days, and all the while life was happening. The plane and this diary and people and relationships and joys and sorrows were all tightly interwoven.

My son's eye surgery was a great success, and today you would never know that anything was ever wrong. My mother-in-law lived with us for three years prior to her death, and our time spent together was enriching for all of us. We have wonderful memories and miss her very much.

2/15/11	Polished half of the rudder. 2 hrs.
2/16/11	Polished the other half of the rudder. 2 hrs.
2/20/11	Started to paint the top and bottom of the rudder's fiberglass parts and the fiberglass tip on the vertical stabilizer. 2 hrs.

2/23/11	Rudder and VS fiberglass tips are sanded and primed. Waiting for the finish paint. Worked on fitting the elevators and getting ready to paint the fiberglass tips on the HS and the elevators. 3 hrs.
2/24/11	Installed additional weight to balance the left elevator. Sanded and primed the HS fiberglass tips. 2 hrs.
2/25/11	Epoxied the elevator tips. 2 hrs.
2/26/11	Sanded and primed the elevator tips. Polished the metal empennage fairings and fitted the left metal fairing with its rubber strip. 5 hrs.
2/27/11	Fitted the right metal empennage fairing with its rubber strip. 2 hrs.
2/28/11	Mated the left wing to the fuselage. Inserted easily. Had to rearrange a few things in the shop. Started to mate the right wing. It did not go in. 3 hrs.
3/1/11	Called Van's and they suggested spreading the fuselage main spar. I needed to spread it 3/64s on the top and 5/64s on the bottom. Finally got the wing on and inserted the temporary bolts. 3 hrs.
3/2/11	Purchased four 7/16 bolts to use for drift pins. Put these temporary bolts in. Started the process of leveling the fuselage perfectly. Pulling measurements off the rear fuselage to the tip of the wings to make sure the measurements are the same. Hung four plumb bobs (2 off of each wing, inboard and outboard) and strung a string across the front of the plane off which to orient the plumb bobs. 3 hrs.
3/3/11	More checking and double-checking the measurements, the sweep, and the incidence of the wing. Finally drilled the critical hole in the rear spar on the left wing. 4 hrs.
3/4/11	Double-checked the measurements on the right wing and drilled the rear spar on the right wing. Drilled ten holes on the underside of each wing that will have screws attaching the fuselage to the wing when the wings are permanently installed. Also, adjusted and drilled the front brace that attaches to the wing fuel tank on each wing. 4 hrs.

Putting the wings on a plane is just flat-out fun! What could possibly make this long, slender, canoe-shaped structure (the fuselage) look more like a plane than to put the wings on? It's also a very important part of the process, because the "sweep and the incidence" of the wing determine how well the plane will fly. One bolt will determine this sweep and incidence, and when you're preparing to drill the hole into which that bolt will fit, you have to be very careful. There are two such bolts—one on each wing—and it actually took me four hours to drill the hole for the first bolt.

I was able to put the wings on by myself, using a small rolling office chair with the back removed. It really worked well, and it wasn't very hard. That was the one bad thing about working in my shop and not being at a hangar. At a hangar I would have had easier access to a helping hand when needed. Most things in life are a compromise, however, and the convenience and savings of working at home far outweighed any of the benefits of being at a hangar.

3/5/11	Put final coat of paint on all empennage tips. Started to permanently install rudder and elevators. 5 hrs.
3/6/11	Purchased and installed difficult top bolt on elevator hinge bracket. My neighbor Ken Moore came over to help by holding a wrench. 1 hr.
3/7/11	Installed lower bolt on elevator hinge bracket. Encountered a problem. My control stick does not operate fully. It hits the top of the seat rib when pushed forward. I started rechecking the length of both of my pushrods. 2 hrs.
3/8/11	Took the flap motor and flap pushrod apart in order to grease the points where the metal rides in the Delrin. Operates much more smoothly. Still trying to figure out why my control stick doesn't have adequate range of motion. Finally talked to Gus at Van's and he said that on the quick-builds, they don't trim the seat ribs. That should be an easy fix tomorrow. 2 hrs.
3/9/11	Trimmed the seat ribs and now the elevators have a full range of motion. Attached, drilled, deburred, finished the edges, trimmed, dimpled, sanded and primed both wing root fairings. 8 hrs.
3/10/11	Cut both holes in the fuselage for the flap pushrods. Built both flap pushrods. Cut the piano hinge wire for both flaps. Fitted the left flap by trimming where the flap rubbed the fuselage. Did most of the fitting for the right flap. 8 hrs.
3/11/11	Finished fitting the right flap. Fabricated two vent pipes for the fuel system from the fuselage to the wings. Took the wings off and put them in their stand. 4 hrs.
3/12/11	Straightened, cut to length, and flared the main fuel lines on both sides of the fuselage. Started to work on the plate nuts that go on the inboard sides of both wings. 3 hrs.
3/13/11	Finished the plate nuts on the inboard sides of both wings. 4 hrs.
3/15/11	Installed the 2 plate nuts on the fore wing tank stabilizers. Dimpled the bottom fuselage skins that attach to the wings. Started to fool around with fitting the fiberglass tips on the wings. 3 hrs.

3/16/11	Fitted the right wing tip. Still have to drill, countersink, and dimple for the plate nuts. 6 hrs.
3/17/11	Drilled, countersunk, and dimpled for the plate nuts on the right wing tip. Trimmed the edge of the left wing tip and started the fitting process. 2 hrs.
3/18/11	Finished work on the left wing tip. Dimpled the metal on the wing where the wing tips attach. 4 hrs.
3/19/11	Epoxied 2 styrofoam blocks in each of the wing tips. This should keep the fiberglass tips from compressing. Drilled the hole and installed the fitting for the pitot tube. Cleaned the shop. Purchased nylon spacers to use for the aileron stops. 5 hrs.
3/20/11	Worked on aileron stops. Started on wing lenses. 2 hrs.
3/21/11	Finished aileron stops. Worked on wing lenses. 2 hrs.
3/22/11	Worked on wing lenses. 2 hrs.
3/23/11	Worked on wing lenses. 2 hrs.
3/24/11	Installed plate nuts for wing lenses. 2 hrs.
3/27/11	For the past couple of days I've been studying the plans and looking at other people's websites in order to begin working on the canopy.
3/28/11	Fabricated the canopy hinge blocks and installed them between the ribs. 3 hrs.

737.5 hours total to this point.

3/31/11	Worked on fitting the canopy hinge. 3 hrs.
4/1/11	Worked on fitting the canopy hinge. Drilled a pilot hole through the hinge blocks and the canopy hinge. 3 hrs.
4/2/11	Worked on canopy. Positioned the skin and drilled holes into the hinge frame. Fitted the brace on the front middle section of hinge frame. 5 hrs.
4/3/11	More canopy hinge frame work. 2 hrs.
4/5/11	The canopy hinge frame is done except for priming, painting, and riveting the skin on. Started to fit the side rails and the aft canopy curved pieces. 4 hrs.
4/6/11	Installed 76 plate nuts on the fiberglass wing tips. Bent the aft canopy curved pieces into shape and rough-fitted the side rails and curved pieces. Fabricated the 704 and the two 613 joiner plates. 5 hrs.
4/7/11	Talked to Ken at Van's about the aft curved canopy pieces. Did more fitting on the side rails. 1 hr.
4/8/11	Drilled, deburred, countersunk, and riveted the side rails onto the canopy hinge frame. 7 hrs.

4/10/11	Visited Nate and Alex in Raleigh this weekend. Worked on cutting the holes in the fuselage for the left side canopy latch and located all of the parts. 1 hr.
4/11/11	Finished cutting and filing holes for canopy latch. Fabricated and finished parts for canopy latch. Riveted canopy latch. 8 hrs.
4/12/11	Tapped canopy latch rod. Primed and painted canopy latch parts. Set up work bench for working on canopy. Taped edges for rough cut on canopy. 8 hrs.
4/13/11	Did rough cut on all four sides of canopy. Set canopy on plane. Took apart 631 frame parts because I ordered new ones last night. 5 hrs.
4/14/11	Fabricated mock-up C-704 part. Clecoed aft skin that goes below rear of canopy. Sat canopy back on. Spent 2 hrs. tonight looking at other builders' sites. 1 hr.
4/16/11	Made big cut on front of canopy. Made big cut to split the canopy. Made several adjustments and small cuts to front of canopy. 8 hrs.

You can see that I'd been working on the canopy for two weeks at this point, and trust me, the fun was just beginning. This was one of the most stressful and tricky parts of the entire build. The stress comes from the fact that the canopy is more fragile and expensive than most individual parts of the plane kit. "So what," you say, "what's so hard?" Well, you have to do a lot of cutting on the canopy, and later you'll be drilling dozens of holes around the perimeter. If these cuts and holes aren't done carefully, you stand a good chance of cracking the canopy and ruining your entire day. The canopy is also one of the most prominent features of the completed plane, and you want it to look right.

The Plexiglas part of the canopy has to be attached to an aluminum frame, and working with the frame is like wrestling a snake. The frame is flimsy, so it's hard to keep it in place until you can finally secure it in the proper position. After that, you have to cut the Plexiglas and fasten it to the frame. (This is where you really start to sweat. If you crack the Plexiglas, you instantly have an expensive piece of nothing, and you have to call up the manufacturer, cry for a few minutes, and order another one.) After you've survived that harrowing experience, you have a lot of tedious fiberglass body work ahead of you in order to make the entire assembly look good. This involves seamlessly blending the Plexiglas to the metal front section of the aluminum frame. I haven't taken the time to count all the hours spent on the canopy—feel free to do it if you like—but I'm sure it'll be close to 200.

4/17/11	Adjusted front of canopy. 2 hrs.
4/18/11	More adjustments on front of canopy. Made long aft cut on rear of canopy. Laid out holes on skin for rear canopy. 6 hrs.
4/19/11	Laid out holes for rear canopy on the roll bar. Started to drill holes for rear canopy. 3 hrs.
4/20/11	Finished the rear canopy. Drilled all holes in the Plexiglas, the skin, and the rollbar. Deburred, dimpled, and countersunk where needed. Also tapped the roll bar with a 6-32 tap so that a #6 screw will fit. 6 hrs.
4/21/11	Reattached the rear skin and rear canopy. Received new C631 parts yesterday, so I bent the top flanges, laid out for screw holes, and fluted the top flanges in order to get the new C631 parts to lie flat. 3 hrs.
4/23/11	More fitting and trimming on the front canopy. Secured front canopy to the roll bar, adjusted the two C631s, and drilled and clecoed the C631s to the WD725s and the F704 plate. Drilled through the front canopy and made marks on the C631s. 6 hrs.
4/24/11	Countersunk and enlarged holes along roll bar on front canopy. Positioned, marked, drilled, and deburred side skirts for front canopy. 4 hrs.
4/25/11	Used side skirts to drill holes in WD725. Also deburred. 1 hr.
4/26/11	Riveted 631 halves together. Drilled, countersunk, and enlarged holes in both sides of the front canopy. 3 hrs.
4/27/11	Countersinking and dimpling on side skirts and 725 sides. Also more fiddling with the C702 skin. 3 hrs.
4/29/11	Had to order another C702 skin. I trimmed the bottom of the original skin too much. Now I have to wait to work further on the canopy. Laid out and drilled the two static port holes. 1 hr.
4/30/11	Installed the two static ports and enough plumbing and supports to get the tubing up into the baggage area. This involved lying in the back area of the plane. Very difficult to get to and to work in. 5 hrs.
5/1/11	Looked at how best to run the static tubing up to the avionics area. Discovered a small problem with how best to install some rivets that were purposefully left out of my quick-build kit. 1 hr.
5/2/11	Solved the rivet problem. Removed the roll bar & shot a few rivets. 1 hr.

5/3/11	Ran the static port tubing up to the avionics area and secured it with adel clamps and homemade metal brackets. Finished fabricating the left-out rivets needed around the bottom of the roll bar attachment points on both sides. 4 hrs.
5/8/11	Sanded roll bar and top edge of fuselage that I had previously painted blue. Taped the area off to paint the top edge of the fuselage. 3 hrs.
5/9/11	Painted the roll bar and the top edge of the fuselage. 2 hrs.
5/11/11	Reinstalled roll bar. 2 hrs.
5/12/11	Purchased NP-1 adhesive and fender washers and permanently installed the aft canopy. Joe Gosnell helped, and we also did about half the riveting on the skin around the aft canopy. 4 hrs.
5/13/11	Joe helped again, and we finished riveting the skin around the aft canopy. Also installed the screws up over the roll bar. Then I clecoed on the front canopy and trimmed the side skirts. 5 hrs.
5/15/11	Started to cut the hole for the canopy latches to fit through. 2 hrs.
5/16/11	Cut the holes for the canopy latches to fit through. 1 hr.
5/17/11	Fitted canopy latches and drilled their holes. 2 hrs.
5/18/11	Sanded, primed, and painted the front canopy skin and side skirts. 2 hrs.
5/20/11	Sanded, primed, and painted the front canopy frame. 2 hrs.
5/21/11	Went to Lynchburg Air Show all day. Blue Angels were there. Getting back to the car was terrible. Poorly organized. Mom and Dad went also.
5/22/11	Painted the canopy roll bar and riveted it onto the canopy frame. Started to rivet the canopy skin on. Edge-finished the three canopy stiffener pieces. 4 hrs.
5/23/11	Dimpled the nine holes in the canopy stiffeners and laid out the location of the stiffeners. 4 hrs.
5/24/11	Worked on attaching the canopy stiffeners. 1 hr.
5/25/11	Drilled, deburred, dimpled, and edge-finished the canopy stiffeners. 3 hrs.
5/26/11	Scotch-brited, primed, and painted the canopy stiffeners. Also deburred the new holes in the canopy top skin and canopy frame. 3 hrs.
5/28/11	Riveted on the canopy stiffeners. 2 hrs.
5/29/11	Riveted on the canopy skin. 4 hrs.
5/30/11	Primed and painted canopy skin. 1 hr.
5/31/11	Sanded off the canopy skin paint and did it again. It was peeling. Also installed the canopy latch parts. 4 hrs.

6/1/11	Installed the front canopy and then screwed and riveted the canopy and the side skirts onto the canopy frame. 5 hrs.
6/2/11	Filed gently on the bottom of the canopy skin where it comes down to the fuselage. Fine-tuned the latching mechanism and the tabs that it latches onto. 3 hrs.
6/4/11	Installed the latching handle inside the canopy. Fabricated the parts for the gas struts that hold the canopy up. 6 hrs.
6/5/11	Drilled and tapped gas strut parts. Primed and painted the gas strut parts after I used the fore parts as guides for drilling the holes in the canopy. 4 hrs.

916.5 hours total to this point.

This is the halfway point. I've got over 900 hours to go, and it will take almost exactly another year and a half before she will fly.

6/6/11	Installed the gas struts. Sanded canopy skin that is outside of the canopy. 4 hrs.
6/7/11	Fabricated and installed 3 small clips to hold down the front of the canopy. Installed electrical tape on the Plexiglas where the finish line is supposed to be. Applied the first layer of thick epoxy and ballons along the bottom edge of the Plexiglas. 3 hrs.
6/8/11	Sanded the first layer of epoxy and then applied a second thinner layer of epoxy. Cut the strips of fabric next. Also sanded the primer off of the fuselage where the steps attach to the fuselage and installed ten more screws on the aft canopy. 4 hrs. Sanded the second layer of epoxy and put on 4 layers of fabric. 2.5 hrs.
6/9/11	Sanded the four layers of fabric and put on 3 more layers. 3 hrs.
6/10/11	Sanded the three layers of fabric. 2 hrs.
6/11/11	Sanded the three layers of fabric with a finer paper. Removed the dust and then brushed on another thin coat of epoxy. Let the epoxy start to firm up and then removed the last layer of electrical tape. 3 hrs.
6/13/11	Fitted the rear strobe and tail light. Fitted the wing tip strobes and navigation lights. 1 hr.
6/14/11	Took the canopy and the two wing tips to Steve Harsh to be painted. Removed the front deck. 1 hr.
6/15/11	Filed the side edges of the skin on the front deck. Sanded, primed, and painted the frame of the front deck. 2 hrs.
6/16/11	Installed and riveted the front deck frame. 3 hrs.

6/18/11	Spent a few hours just looking at the plans and figuring out how things go through and get placed on the firewall. Drilled holes and added plate nuts for the battery case, the master relay, and the starter relay. Also relocated the brake master cylinder, which I had installed five years ago. 3 hrs.
6/21/11	Spent a little time soldering wires to the trim servo. 1 hr.
6/22/11	Made up Molex connector for the aft strobe and marker light. The male end was soldered improperly. 2 hrs.
6/23/11	Met Jason Moorefield at the Lynchburg airport. He heads up the avionics department. He fixed my male Molex. I may get him to help me with avionics.

Jason proved to be one of my main helpers on the plane. I knew that I'd need some help when it came to the avionics portion of the build, and I proved it when I first tried to wire a simple Molex connector. I messed it up. Jason's been working at the Lynchburg Regional Airport for years and is very good at what he does. He was quick to explain how I had fouled up the Molex—he even fixed it for me right on the spot—and he was willing to come out to my shop and work when I needed help. I ended up pulling almost all of the wires for the plane and connecting most of the ends (successfully), but only because Jason had invested many hours of patient instruction into the project. He even lent me tools several times, and helped with other phases of the build, not just the electrical work. Thanks, Jason!

6/27/11	Ordered GTX 327, SL 40, and TRU TRAK EFIS.
6/28/11	Wired up the rear marker light and strobe and wired up the trim servo. 4 hrs.
6/29/11	Fabricated a heat sink/mounting bracket for the rear marker light. Pulled the wires for the rear marker light and the trim servo up to the firewall. Installed the rear marker light. 8 hrs.
6/30/11	Installed the trim servo. Installed another nut plate and adel clamp for the ELT cable which goes to the antenna in the rear of the fuselage. Wired up all wires for the right wing marker light and strobe and half of the left wing marker light. Installed both wing marker lights. 8 hrs.
7/2/11	Mounted all three tires. Wired a little bit of the left wing. Cut access holes in the fuselage conduit. Installed the dynafocal engine mount. 8 hrs.

7/3/11	Drilled the hole in the firewall that allows installation of the bolt that secures the front gear leg to the engine mount. Filed and sanded the holes so that everything fits on the installation of the gear legs. 2 hrs.
7/4/11	Refitted my main tires in order to line up the red dot with the valve stem. Figured out and then installed the U-403 brake bracket, the brake attachment plate, and the wheels. Drilled holes in the axle for the cotter pin that secures the wheel nut. 8 hrs.
7/5/11	Worked on panel layout. 2 hrs.
7/6/11	Picked up the SL 40 and the GTX 327 from Jason at Virginia Aviation.
7/8/11	Packed all six wheel bearings with new Aeroshell #5 grease. 2 hrs.
7/9/11	Finished mounting front wheel. Done except for wheel pants. Pulled wires for both AP servos. Pulled wires in left wing for navigation & strobe lights. Pulled tubing for pitot through wing and determined best way to route tube to the EFIS on the panel. 6 hrs.
7/11/11	Dinked around this morning and didn't really get much done. I intended to install Molex connectors at the wing root, but I think I'll wait and talk to Jason. Tied wires together in the right wing and prepared to rivet the right wing skin on. Did a little work on running the pitot tube from the wing into the cabin. 2 hrs.
7/12/11	Decided to work on the right wing while I'm waiting for the TruTrak EFIS. Set up a tent for shade, put the wing on a dolly table so I can move it by myself, figured out how to install the last skin, and washed the top of the wing. 3 hrs.
7/13/11	Polished half of the top side of the right wing. Changed out 5 bolts that secure the right landing gear weldment. The 12A bolts were too short. 6 hrs.
7/14/11	Changed out 6 bolts that secure the left landing gear weldment. 1 hr.
7/15/11	Polished the second half of the top side of the right wing. 3 hrs.
7/16/11	Polished half of the bottom of the right wing. Installed the 5A bolts in each of the main wheel-to-brake-bracket assemblies. 5 hrs.
7/21/11	Left to visit Wynne & Vickie and to go to Oshkosh. Wynne & Vickie went with us on Tuesday the 26th. Returned home on the 28th.
8/4/11	Jason Moorefield came to the shop. Showed him what I've done. He made a list of additional avionics parts to order. Installed Molex connectors at wing root. Concerned about splicing the shielded wire to the strobe lights. 2 hrs.
8/6/11	Installed Molex connectors on wires coming from the fuselage and going into the wings. 5 hrs.
8/9/11	Jason came to the shop (3.5). Jason wired SL 40 and GTX 327. I drilled holes for headphone jacks and routing of headphone wires and GPS antenna. 4 hrs.
8/10/11	Mounted Garmin GPS antenna and pulled GPS antenna wire and headphone wires. 3 hrs.

8/11/11 Cut holes in panel for SL 40, GTX 327, and AERA 510. Added angle bracing on the sides of the cut-out. 6 hrs.

8/12/11 Cut hole for the long SL 40 in the sub-panel behind the panel. 2 hrs.

8/13/11 Added brace to hole cut for SL 40. Drilled holes for mounting the transponder and comm antennas. Pulled both antenna wires. 5 hrs.

1,049 hours total to this point.

8/15/11 Put antenna wire for comm and Xponder in conduit. Tied up some electrical loose ends. 2 hrs.

8/16/11 Figured out a way to flush-mount the iFly700 to the panel by using the existing suction mount; laid out the three round gauges. 2 hrs.

8/17/11 Added small ledge support for iFly700. 2 hrs.

8/18/11 Laid out and cut the hole, drilled the attach point holes, and added the plate nuts for screws that hold the TruTrak EFIS. 3 hrs.

8/27/11 Went to EAA cookout in Roanoke. Pulled pitch servo wire. Cut metal bracket that holds throttle and fuel mixture. Started mounting pitch servo motor. 4 hrs.

8/28/11 Adusted pitch servo wire. Drilled holes in firewall for throttle cable, mixture cable, and fuel line. 2 hrs.

9/3/11 Cut out two square holes, punched out three round holes, and drilled one small hole in panel. Decided to keep AP servo in left wing. 2 hrs.

For some homebuilders, the instrument panel is their favorite part of building a plane. It's one of the most visible parts—after checking out the paint scheme, everyone then looks in at the panel—and after the control stick and the throttle, it's the part you interact with most closely. I can't say that this was really my favorite job (mostly because I'm not an electrical guy), but it was definitely rewarding to step back and look at a panel that was symmetrical, well organized, clearly labeled, and functionally efficient.

9/4/11 Mounted pitch servo motor. 4 hrs.

9/5/11 Installed Molex on new roll servo wires at wing root. Made list of all electrical items on plane. 2 hrs.

9/6/11 Fabricated bracket and input fuel line for electric fuel pump after determining the best location for installation. 3 hrs.

9/7/11 Drilled, deburred, and dimpled for fuel pump bracket. 1 hr.

9/8/11 Fabricated doubler for comm antenna and fuel line through firewall. Drilled, deburred, dimpled, and primed both pieces. 2 hrs.

9/12/11	Fabricated fuel line from valve to electric fuel pump. 2 hrs.
9/17/11	Worked on cover for electric fuel pump. Looked at best way to route wires to panel. 2 hrs.

Since this was my first plane project, I didn't deviate from the plans. I would never have trusted myself to do something like that on anything structural or anything that would remotely affect the flight characteristics of the plane. However, there were several opportunities to add some of my own personal touches, and the cover for the electric fuel pump was one of the small items that I got to design. I was quite proud of it!

9/19/11	Installed AP servo in left wing. 2 hrs.
9/20/11	Drilled hole for starter switch in panel. 1 hr.
9/21/11	Secured electric fuel pump in position after attaching 2 wires. Installed AN fitting for fuel line where it goes through the firewall. Looked at panel for placement of switches and circuit breakers. Redid wires for right wing from fuselage Molex to panel. 4 hrs.
9/22/11	Finished laying out and drilling holes in panel. Finished attach points for radio trays. Attached throttle and mixture bracket with nut plates. 4.5 hrs.
9/24/11	Fabricated battery holding box. Did holes and plate nuts for fuel pump cover. Painted panel and fuel pump cover. 4 hrs.
9/25/11	Installed battery box. Installed master & starter solenoids. 4 hrs.
9/26/11	Fabricated copper bars from master to starter solenoids and installed them. Put brake lines on master cylinder and pedal cylinders. 3 hrs.
9/27/11	Fabricated and installed fuel line from electric pump to firewall fitting. Hooked up all fuel lines coming out of fuel valve. Finished installing brake lines. Started putting avionics onto the panel. 4 hrs.
9/28/11	Put all avionics onto the panel except for a few switches. Hooked up pitot and static tubing. Determined best way to route wires. Installed plate nuts on sub-panel for holding adel clamps for wires. 5 hrs.
9/29/11	Still working on wires. 2 hrs.
9/30/11	Changed breakers to 1 amp for Ray Allen trim servo & indicator. Fabricated and installed two copper bars for circuit breaker power source. 2 hrs.
10/1/11	Still working on wires for panel. 8 hrs.

10/3/11	Wired up rocker switch and panel light for elevator trim. 4 hrs.
10/4/11	Went to airport to talk with Jason & Jake about wire size and wire hookup for wire that goes from the master solenoid to the main bus. 1 hr.
10/8/11	Installed ground bus and wired up several wires to connect to ground bus. Changed direction of 5 plate nuts. 3 hrs.
10/9/11	Wired up Aero LED lights to CB, ground bus, and switch. Wired two other items to CB. 2 hrs.
10/13/11	Borrowed large terminal crimper from Jason Moorefield and fabricated and installed #6 wire from starter to main bus. Installed wires from main bus to switch to avionics bus. 2 hrs.
10/15/11	Jason Moorefield came over at 7:15 a.m. Wired Xponder, installed AERA GPS, and put BNC connectors on antenna cable. 3 hrs.
10/16/11	Wired flap switch, connected transponder wires to CB, and connected iFly GPS to CB. 2.5 hrs.
10-22-11	Jason come over at 7:15 a.m. Finished transponder, wired starter and master switch, figured out wires to EFIS and EMS, and wired toggle switch for EFIS. 6 hrs.
10/24/11	Started to tie wires together. 1 hr.
10/25/11	Continued to tie wires together. 1 hr.
10/27/11	Realized that I had been sent the old instruction sheet for my TruTrak EFIS harness from SteinAir and that a couple of wires that I had already done were wrong. Between looking at the manual and undoing a bunch of wire ties, a fair amount of time was wasted. 3 hrs.
10/28/11	Corresponded with SteinAir and redid some wires. 5 hrs.
10/29/11	Hooked up wires to pitch AP servo. 1 hr.
10/30/11	Hooked up wires to roll AP servo. 1 hr.
11/6/11	Finished installation of roll AP servo. Drilled holes, installed grommets, and pulled wires to leave in wings if I ever want to add lights later. 6 hrs.
11/8/11	Started riveting on last bottom wing skin of the right wing. This is hard to do by yourself. 2 hrs.
11/9/11	Finished riveting the skin on the right wing. 4 hrs.
11/16/11	Started riveting on last bottom wing skin of the left wing. 1 hr.
11/17/11	Finished riveting the skin on the left wing. 4.5 hrs.
11/19/11	Lifted the fuselage and empennage with engine hoist off of the stand that the plane has been on for the past few years, and installed the main gear and wheels. Also bolted on the engine mount and the front gear and wheel. Still a lot to do but it really looks great. 3 hrs.

1,181.5 hours total to this point.

Some builders like to get their plane up on its gear as quickly as possible. It looks like a plane then, and makes you feel as though you've accomplished something. However, there is a big practical drawback to doing that—the fuselage is now higher, and it's much harder to reach in and work on the cockpit and the instrument panel. Another builder suggested keeping the fuselage on low sawhorses for as long as possible, especially until the panel is done. I would strongly agree. Nevertheless, I must admit, the "cool" factor was very high when, after eight years of sitting low, the plane was finally standing on its own three legs.

An engine hoist can also be used to lift the fuselage when it's time to put the legs on.

11/24/11	My brother Rob helped me do rivets on the right wing, the AP pitch servo bracket, and the ELT bracket. 0.5 hr.
11/27/11	Cut the 2-inch hole in the firewall for the cabin heater. 0.5 hr.
12/4/11	Jason Moorefield came over (4 hrs.) and answered the remaining avionics questions. We wired up the headphone jacks, he figured out the loose EFIS wires, and I pulled wires for the fuel gauges and the push-to-talk switch on the pilot control stick. Also, I later bent the fuel sender float wires and installed them, and I installed the outside air temperature (OAT) probe. 8 hrs.
12/7/11	Started to fabricate a cover plate for the metal bracket above the baggage area. I ran my headset wires to this bracket and now I need to hide the wires. 0.5 hrs.
12/8/11	Finished fabricating the cover plate; drilled, deburred, dimpled and installed 10 plate nuts on the bracket to hold the cover plate. 3 hrs.

12/10/11	Primed and painted the two air scoops and my newly fabricated cover plate. 1 hr.
12/11/11	Installed the two air scoops on the left and right sides of the front fuselage. 1 hr.
12/12/11	Installed the cover plate over the headphone jacks. Primed and painted the middle fuselage fore floor cover plate. 1 hr.
12/13/11	Installed the flap motor and right side cover. Figured out a way to take the slop out of the pilot control stick. Works perfectly now. Also drove to Fincastle today to talk with Bob Barrows about building an engine. 2 hrs.
12/14/11	Spent time talking with James at J&J Airparts about Superior engines and asking Bob Howell, Jason Moorefield, and Joey about using Glenn Lacey as a builder.
12/18/11	Firewall forward kit arrived. Inventoried parts. 2 hrs.
12/22/11	Safety wired the AN 818-6D coupling nuts on the fuel tank pickup tubes and installed the T-408 cover plates. 1.5 hrs.
12/31/11	Jason Moorefield came over. Finished cockpit side of EFIS wires, installed current meter, rewired AERA GPS. 4 hrs.
1/2/12	Used my new Brother labelmaker to label the panel; 95% is done and it looks pretty good. 3 hrs.
1/7/12	Looked at firewall forward plans. Installed transducer on firewall and removed heater box. Doug and Steve came over from Roanoke and inspected my work thus far. (They've built a 9-A and restored a Cessna 180; and Steve is an A&P.) 2 hrs.
1/8/12	Installed the brake calipers and started to install the heater box cable. 2 hr.
1/9/12	Finished installing heater box cable and adjusted the middle cover panel. 2 hrs.
1/10/12	Flew up to Altoona, PA, in John Poyner's RV 8. John took Dad for a ride above Altoona and even found their home in Greenwood. Got to Altoona from Roanoke in only 1 hour and 15 minutes. Great day of flying. Finished adjusting the middle cover panel in the cockpit directly aft of the firewall when I got back home. 1 hr.
1/13/12	Determined proper positioning of the LORD engine mounts. Installed rubber mounts, washers, and bolts, and then put tape around them to keep everything in place. 2 hrs.
1/15/12	Installed 45 and 90 degree fittings into transducer; then installed 2 plate nuts on the firewall to hold the oil pressure hose. 2 hrs.
1/16/12	Fabricated 2 small angle brackets and labeled the throttle, mixture, and cabin heat cables. 1 hr.
1/22/12	Gail helped me position both of the wings so that I can join the Molex connectors and test the wing tip lights and strobes. Inserted into a Molex one right-wing grounding wire. 1 hr.

1/23/12	Studied cowlings and cowling fastener systems online for almost 2 hrs.
1/24/12	Connected a battery and fired up the plane's electrical system. Navigation lights, strobes, avionics, radios, flap motor, starter switch, and elevator trim motor all worked fine, and there was no smoke. Set up the right wing on a table in order to continue polishing. This time I've covered the shop floor in the polishing area. I saw that I had forgotten a cotter pin on the pilot's brakes. Installed that pin and then labeled the switch that changes the TruTrak glass panel from EFIS to EMS. 3 hrs.

I might change my mind and decide that the panel really is my favorite part of plane-building after all. Turning on all that fancy equipment for the first time and having the lights, the electric motors, the electronic avionics, and all those switches work just the way they were supposed to was shockingly fun (pun intended).

1/26/12	Polished on underside of right wing. 1.5 hrs.
1/28/12	Met David Miller at nearby New London Airport at 10 a.m. to talk about hangars. Open hangar is $78 per month and enclosed is $145. Met CP, an A&P who works at Lynchburg and New London. Finished polishing underside of right wing and rebuffed the top of the right wing. Right wing is done. Installed clear Plexiglas on wing tips. 5 hrs.
1/29/12	CJ came over and helped me put the polished right wing back in the wing cradle; then we took the left wing outside, washed it, brought it back inside, and set it up to be polished. Compounded 25% of the underside. 3 hrs.
1/30/12	Finished compounding the underside of the left wing. 3 hrs.
2/1/12	Finished polishing the underside of the left wing and started compounding the top side of the left wing. 3 hrs.
2/2/12	More compounding on the top side of the left wing. 1.5 hrs.
2/3/12	Finished compounding and polishing the top side of the left wing. 4.5 hrs.
2/4/12	Bob Howell from LU's A&P program came to see the plane today. Washed the flaps and ailerons and then compounded both ailerons. Also, installed a little clip on the passenger control stick to hold it in place. 4 hr.
2/6/12	Polished both ailerons. Compounded both flaps and polished one flap. 3 hrs.
2/7/12	Finished polishing the second flap. Cleaned up the shop. 1 hr.

1,257 hours total to this point.

2/8/12	Installed aileron and flap onto left wing. 2 hrs.
2/9/12	Installed aileron and flap onto right wing. 2 hrs.
2/11/12	Put firesleeve on wire bundle and mixture cable penetrations of firewall. Washed half of fuselage and put sheets over parts of fuselage in preparation for polishing fuselage. 3 hrs.

I would be afraid to total all the hours that I put into compounding and polishing this plane. I really like the result, but it's a hard, nasty job!

2/12/12	Compounded part of rear fuselage. 1.5 hrs.
2/13/12	Compounded rest of rear fuselage. 1.5 hrs.
2/14/12	Polished part of rear fuselage. 1 hr.
2/18/12	Polished rest of rear fuselage. Washed front half of fuselage and put sheets in place. 4 hrs.
2/19/12	Compounded left side of front fuselage. 2 hrs.
2/20/12	Polished left side of front fuselage. Compounded right side of front fuselage. 3 hrs.
2/21/12	Washed underside of fuselage and compounded 30% of underside of fuselage. It's not easy lying on your back and holding the tools straight out. 3 hrs.
2/22/12	Polished right side of front fuselage. 1 hr.
2/23/12	Compounded another 50% of underside of fuselage. I really don't like doing this. 4 hrs.
2/24/12	Finished compounding underside of fuselage. 1.5 hrs.
2/25/12	Polished underside of fuselage. Picked up all of the sheets and tarps on the garage floor. Vacuumed garage floor. Got engine hoist and tractor forks ready for engine to arrive. 5 hrs.
2/27/12	The Superior engine was delivered by Estes Trucking today around 2 p.m. Unloaded it, uncrated it, and got it on the hoist. Installed a few plugs on the rear that would be hard to access when the engine is installed. Put 1 engine bolt in. 3 hrs.

One of the major milestones of any plane-building project is the arrival of the engine. For a week or more I'd been reading the instructions (and other builders' websites) to ascertain the best procedure for "hanging an engine." Everyone's not in agreement, and even though there are only four bolts securing the engine to the engine mount, the sequence of installing those bolts is still controversial. Oh, well—either approach will get the job done!

The standard joke among homebuilders is that once you reach the "firewall forward" portion of the project (the engine), you are 90% done with only 90% to go. A bit of wry humor! In reality, at this point I had about two thirds of the job completed.

I could tell you more about my choice of engine here, but books have been written on the subject, so suffice it to say that I went with a standard aircraft engine. Those interested in building will spend a lot of time reading about engines even if they know from the beginning that they intend to go with a typical engine. There are many options. If you intend to go "nontypical," then all bets are off (as far as time goes), and I wish you good luck. I read about one guy who became so frustrated with his nontypical engine that he eventually gave up, sold his project, and bought a plane.

The engine is hung.

2/28/12	Worked the second engine bolt in. 1 hr.
2/29/12	Finally got the third and fourth bolts installed, tightened down all four bolts and cotter-pinned all four bolts. Studied diagrams for hooking up throttle and mixture cables. 3 hrs.
3/3/12	Connected fuel hose from firewall to fuel pump. Connected fuel hose from fuel pump to injector. Connected hose from fuel pump to fuel transducer. Installed fuel overflow tube. Installed oil breather tube. Installed the exhaust system. Nathen & Alex came to visit, and Nathan helped a few hours with the exhaust parts. 8.5 hrs.
3/4/12	Installed the alternator. Started to work on heat muff, and that led to laying out the baffle parts to see how they interconnect. 3 hrs.

3/5/12	Looked at Mike Bullock's website to pick up a few tips on engine injection systems for a couple of hours. Installed prop spacer on prop and deburred the aft spinner bulkhead. Drilled holes and deburred the fore spinner bulkhead. 2 hrs.
3/6/12	Installed the prop, then covered it with plastic and put protective foam on both tips to protect both it and me. Looked some more at the heat muff. 1 hr.

The prop and the engine were both on, so this thing should be flying any day now, right? Not quite. There are still several months to go. In fact, the top and bottom cowl that I would be pulling off the shelf tomorrow would require almost as much time as the canopy.

3/7/12	Pulled the top cowl off the shelf and started fitting. 3 hrs.
3/8/12	Trimmed aft end of top cowl. Trying to figure out oil access door. 3 hrs.
3/12/12	Finished oil access door, but I didn't rivet on the hinge. Sanded aft end of top cowl. Cut and cecloed to the firewall the two pieces of top hinge. 3 hrs.
3/13/12	Cut and fit two pieces of .020 metal shim for the two top hinges. Riveted on the two top hinges to the firewall. Continued to fit top cowl. Angled several of the hinge eyes on the top hinge section that attaches to the cowl. 4 hrs.
3/14/12	Fit, drilled, and clecoed the top cowl to the two hinge sections. Made shims; also drilled, countersunk, and deburred the two side hinge sections. Riveted the two side hinges to the firewall. Cut out the middle strip area on the bottom cowl. Made shims and drilled, countersunk, and deburred the two bottom hinges. 8 hrs.
3/15/12	Riveted two bottom hinges to the firewall. Looked at bottom cowl. Fit top and bottom cowl together on the workbench. 2 hrs.
3/17/12	Working on fitting top and bottom cowls. 2 hrs.
3/18/12	Still working on fitting top and bottom cowls. 5 hrs.
3/19/12	Called Van's this morning and spoke with Ken. He said that I am being too picky worrying about the fact that my cowl opening around the spinner is not centered left to right. Trimmed aft sides and bottom of bottom cowl. Clecoed aft sides and bottom hinges to the bottom cowl. Started trimming the seam between top and bottom cowl. 7 hrs.
3/20/12	Steven Brinly came over tonight and spent a couple of hours looking at the plane and answering several of my questions. He will be a big help.

I met Steven and his wife Whitney through one of my businesses. He is a multitalented guy who is an A&P *and* a CFI, so he can both fix a plane and teach you how to fly it. I had an immediate need for one of his talents, and I hoped that in the not-too-distant future I'd be taking advantage of the other talent. He had shown an interest in my project when we first met, and I appreciated his coming over to check everything out.

3/21/12	Fabricated the bottom metal bracket that supports the middle of the cowl. 1 hr.
3/22/12	Worked some more on those bottom metal bracket supports. Started working on the hinges that connect top and bottom cowls. 3 hrs.
3/23/12	My cowl was too close to the ring gear on the left side. Started fitting cowl again. Ended up with a gap on the right side between cowl and fuselage, but I can fix that with epoxy. 3 hrs.
3/24/12	Drilled all new holes for all the firewall-to-cowl hinges. Sanded seam between top and bottom cowl. Fabricated hinges between top and bottom cowl. Drilled cowl seam hinges to the bottom cowl. 8 hrs.
3/25/12	Drilled cowl seam hinges to the top cowl. Countersunk holes in top cowl. Deburred and primed all hinges that attach to the top cowl. 5 hrs.
3/26/12	Epoxied and riveted, and then cleaned up the mess I made with the epoxy on all hinges of the top cowl. Countersunk side seams of bottom cowl; deburred and primed side hinges of bottom cowl. Epoxied and riveted side seam hinges to bottom cowl. Didn't make a mess this time. 8 hrs.
3/27/12	Finished bottom hinges on bottom cowl. 1 hr.
3/29/12	Started taping fuselage off in order to try to fill gap between cowl and fuselage with epoxy. 3 hrs.
3/30/12	Epoxied cowl and fuselage gap. 2 hrs.
3/31/12	Added mesh fabric to cowl and fuselage gap. 2 hrs.
4/1/12	Sanded some on top and bottom of cowl gap repairs. Fabricated and mounted throttle bracket. Installed firewall penetration and fire shield for throttle. 5 hrs.
4/2/12	Finished installing throttle. Started working on mixture bracket and bell crank. 2 hrs.
4/3/12	Borrowed neighbor Ken's Dremel tool and cleaned the excess epoxy around all of the cowl piano hinges. 1 hr.
4/4/12	Finished cleaning around piano hinges and refitted cowls. 1 hr.

4/5/12	Modified mixture bracket and mounted that. Started looking at angle for the bell crank. Inverted the mixture arm on the controller. 2 hrs.
4/6/12	Got everything to fit on mixture bracket and cable. 2 hrs.
4/7/12	Finished mixture bracket and cable. Put protective pieces on fuel line below mixture bracket. Riveted the front top fuselage skin with Nathan's help. Tedious to get bucking bar in position while lying on your back under the panel. 7 hrs.
4/8/12	Used Ken's Dremel tool again for a small hinge section. Installed 6 nut plates on the front nose of the lower cowl. 1 hr.
4/9/12	Applied a bit more epoxy to the fuselage edge of both the top and bottom cowl. Sorted and labeled baffle parts. 2 hrs.
4/10/12	Separated and edge-finished several baffle parts. Started putting together the aft #4 cylinder area of baffles, which included cutting the opening for the oil cooler. Drilled, deburred, dimpled some, and edge-finished most of these parts. 6 hrs.
4/11/12	Started putting together the aft #3 cylinder area of baffles. 2 hrs.
4/12/12	Sanded, primed, and riveted braces and backing plates of baffles. Mounted fore and aft baffle support brackets on the engine. 2.5 hrs.
4/13/12	Worked on left and right side baffles. 2.5 hrs.
4/14/12	Worked on left and right baffle front ramps. Not going to be easy. 4 hrs.
4/15/12	Today is Sunday, and I relaxed. Made up a small parts list to order.

"The baffles are truly baffling," as the corny saying goes, but truer words were never spoken. This part was hard! I really did spend this entire week looking at other builders' websites in an effort to understand how all the parts in a horizontal induction system are supposed to fit together.

4/21/12	Not much accomplished this past week in the shop, but I spent a lot of hours on the computer trying to figure out how the air filter, filter air box, and baffles all come together. Fitted and trimmed the snorkel today; also fine-tuned the rear bulkheads and installed the ignition wire pass-through plastic pieces. 7 hrs.
4/22/12	Worked on fitting the left front baffle ramp to the FAB. 3 hrs.
4/23/12	Cut the opening out of the left front baffle ramp for the FAB. 2 hrs.
4/25/12	Had to adjust the opening and then worked on the metal pieces that attach the FAB to the left baffle ramp. 2 hrs.
4/26/12	All day and not much to show for it. Finally got the left ramp with FAB attachment mostly done. 8 hrs.

4/27/12	Worked on right baffle ramp and right cylinder baffle. 6 hrs.
4/28/12	Worked on right crankcase baffle and the right conical piece. Had to trim inboard lower cowl ears on both sides of cowl. 6 hrs.
4/29/12	Worked on left crankcase baffle. 4 hrs.
5/2/12	Figured out a way to install a left conical baffle piece and worked on that. 1.5 hrs
5/3/12	Finished left conical piece and fabricated a small piece for both left and right ramp front edges. 1.5 hrs.
5/4/12	Started to take the front ramps apart. Drilled parts where needed and added plate nuts where needed; deburred, smoothed edges, and did sanding and priming. 1.5 hrs.
5/5/12	Finished taking the baffles apart, drilled and deburred where needed, sanded and primed all parts, and then started to rivet cylinder 1 and right ramp baffles. 6 hrs.
5/6/12	Finished riveting right ramp and left ramp baffles to the cylinder 1 and 3 baffles and to the front right and left crankcase baffles. Installed on engine. 4 hrs.
5/8/12	Riveted together the 2 and 4 baffles and then installed them on the engine. Then raised the top cowl and made the preliminary cut mark. 6 hrs.
5/9/12	Made the preliminary cut on the baffles. Worked well. Put paper clips on the back row of baffles and Gail helped me gently put the top cowl on and then take it off. Seemed to work very well. Marked for final cut and then put more paper clips on the side baffles. 3 hrs.
5/10/12	Cut the back baffles. Put paper clips on the side and front baffles and then marked all of that. Then cut the side and front baffles. 6 hrs.
5/11/12	Gail had her right foot reconstructed today by Dr. Wisbeck; a 5-hr surgery.
5/12/12	More baffle marking and trimming. Also placed and clecoed the plastic front ramps that go on the top cowl. 3 hrs.
5/14/12	Adjusted plastic front ramps, sanded everything, and epoxied front ramps in place. 2 hrs.

1,498.5 hours total to this point.

5/17/12	Mixed up microballoon filler and put it on front ramps. 1 hr.
5/18/12	Put expanding foam under front ramps and in between the ramps in order to shape the cowl to fit the front baffles. 3 hrs.
5/19/12	Sculpted the expanding foam to shape. Applied first layer of fabric and epoxy over the foam. Saw that I had cut the front side baffles incorrectly and started to fix them. 6 hrs.

5/20/12 Applied a second layer of fabric and epoxy. Fabricated pieces to fix the error on the side baffles. Used paper clip trick on the front ramp area of the side baffles and trimmed these baffles. Applied three layers of fabric and epoxy on the hole in the snorkel. Made backer plates for the pieces that attach to the top of the snorkel. Riveted these pieces and the plates on. 8 hrs.

5/21/12 Made one more adjustment cut-and-patch on snorkel. 1 hr.

5/22/12 Used acetone to dissolve the styrofoam in the snorkel. This left a mess. Took awhile to clean up. 1 hr.

5/23/12 CJ's birthday. He and Megan brought pizza and a cake to our place.

In case you're one of those people who read all the fine print, I'd better explain why my son and his girlfriend had to bring pizza and cake over to our house for *his* birthday. Did you notice that on 5/11/12 my wife had her right foot reconstructed? It was a major operation—two doctors, five hours—and it had her laid up for several weeks. We usually do a better job on birthdays.

5/24/12 Used epoxy to level off problem area in snorkel and do some patching on the cowl ramps. More trimming on front crankcase baffles. Fabricated pieces and installed plate nuts for the two small trim pieces on both side of the baffles. Installed paper clips one more time for a final check all around. 6 hrs.

5/26/12 Paper clip trick indicated that the left side closest to the cockpit needed about 4 inches trimmed and a little bit of touch-up on a couple other areas. Finished that trimming. Fabricated the rods that secure the bottom of the baffles. 3 hrs.

5/27/12 Finished the baffle rods. Nathan helped. Started cutting and installing the rubber baffle seals. Finished left and right sides. 5 hrs.

5/28/12 Cut and installed rear baffle seals. Worked on trimming the left and right outboard front baffle seals. Started fitting crankcase baffle seals. 3 hrs.

5/29/12 Finished crankcase baffle seals. Did right lower cowl seal. 4 hrs.

5/30/12 Did left lower cowl seal. Steve Brinly came over, and he routed the starter cable. Cut hole for heat duct intake. Looked at how to fit heat duct. 3 hrs.

5/31/12 Saw Jason Moorefield and picked up a grounding strap and borrowed a large crimping tool. Installed ends and finished starter wire. Installed ends and attached grounding wire from grounding block to engine. Adjusted #3 baffle and then primed and painted it.

	Removed and started to adjust #4 baffle. Added stiffeners on #4 baffle for oil cooler. 6 hrs.
6/1/12	Started routing alternator wires. 2 hrs.
6/2/12	Painted #4 baffle. Installed #3 baffle. Changed out some adel clamps and screws. Painted snorkel. Vacuumed and blew off engine. 5 hrs.
6/4/12	Installed top spark plug wire guides. Added a couple of adel clamps. 2 hrs.
6/5/12	Installed plate nut and adel clamp behind #4 cylinder for lower left spark plug wires. Installed adel clamp for lower right spark plug wires. Fabricated another bracket for oil cooler. Started installing oil cooler. 2 hrs.
6/6/12	Installed oil cooler and oil cooler hoses. Installed blast tubes to magnetos. 2 hrs.
6/7/12	Worked on lower cowl baffle seals. 1 hr.
6/10/12	Used Pliobond to glue lower cowl baffle seals. Primed and painted both front baffle sections. 3 hrs.
6/11/12	Made bracket to support 60 amp alternator breaker. Worked on fitting left and right air vents. Reattached fuel vent lines inside front fuselage. 3 hrs.
6/12/12	Steve Brinly came over and answered several questions. Installed the CHT fittings. Applied RTV and riveted on the right baffle seals. 2.5 hrs.
6/13/12	Started to route wires for EGT, CHT, and spark plugs and installed adel clamps. 1.5 hrs.
6/14/12	Almost finished routing wires for EGT, CHT, and spark plugs. Lots of adel clamps and calls to Jason Moorefield and Steve Brinly. Hooked up mag leads. 9 hrs.
6/16/12	Finished routing EGT & CHT wires. Installed front left baffles. Fabricated the left outer tension rod and installed all four tension rods. 4 hrs.
6/17/12	Installed left baffle seals and front baffle seals. Started to install interior fuselage air vents. Looked at how to attach alternator wire to breaker and bus. 3 hrs.
6/18/12	Finished connecting the alternator wire to the 60-amp breaker and then to the main bus. Finished connecting the right interior air vent. 1 hr.
6/19/12	Started working on left interior air vent. 1 hr.
6/20/12	Adjusted left interior air vent. 0.5 hr.
6/21/12	Finished left interior air vent. Finished hooking up alternator switch and 5-amp breaker. Installed snorkel. 3.5 hrs.
6/22/12	Started looking at how to route fuel-flow sensor. Thought I could do it inside the fuselage. Cannot. 1 hr.

6/23/12	Figured out how to route fuel-flow sensor (FWF). Drilled drain hole in snorkel. Fabricated and installed the rear bracket that supports the aft lower cowl. 8 hrs.
6/24/12	Gary & Joan Wooldridge, Larry Roberts, & Charles Roberts came over this afternoon to look at the plane. Charles built a single-seater from plans back in 1975 to 1978. Put a few rivets in the bottom of the firewall. 0.5 hrs.
6/26/12	Installed fuel-flow sensor and fuel lines. Secured all of this with adel clamps. Started to look at installation of heat muff on #1 cylinder and the routing of the scat tubing. 3 hrs.
6/27/12	Installed heat muff and scat tubes from the baffle flange to the cockpit heater box. 2 hrs.
	1,609 hours total to this point.

I don't know if you're tired from looking at this lengthy chapter yet or not, but by this point in the project, I was feeling both tired and exhilarated at the same time—worn out, but motivated by the fact that we were in the home stretch. This pile of parts was starting to look like a plane.

7/4/12	Power was off due to a very bad windstorm from 6-29 to 7-3. Hard to work in the shop without electricity. Fabricated a bracket and installed a small scat tube to cool the alternator. Reinstalled the prop and fitted the cowling. Fabricated hinge pins for the lowest firewall hinges. Sanded on cowl a bit at the fore corners. 3 hrs.
7/5/12	Started to put epoxy on the front of the cowl in order to get an even space between the spinner and the cowl. Installed canopy as the epoxy set. 4 hrs.
7/6/12	Had to take the prop and prop spacer apart so that I could reshape the aft spinner backing plate. Hit my thumb when doing this. Not easy to get apart. 2 hrs.
7/7/12	Will have to return prop spacer to Sensenich to be checked. Made a wooden spacer to use temporarily. Worked on cutting spinner to fit around prop. 4 hrs.
7/8/12	Made both big cuts on the spinner. Both fit great. 1 hr.
7/9/12	Riveted nut plates on the aft spinner backer plate. Made a template and cut out one of the filler pieces. 1.5 hrs.
7/11/12	Cut out the second filler piece and sanded one of them. 1 hr.

7/13/12	Finished final sanding on both filler pieces and spinner cutouts. Made two small backer plates for filler pieces out of .063 aluminum. 3 hrs.
7/14/12	Finished all nut plates. Countersunk holes on spinner. Riveted backer plates to filler pieces. Mixed small batch of epoxy and put on cowling. Installed isolater washers on headset receptacles. 7 hrs.
7/15/12	Reinstalled prop and spinner temporarily and worked on distance between spinner and cowling. 3 hrs.
7/22/12	Nathan helped remove that bolt from the aft elevator bell crank and reinstall it with an additional flat washer and lock washer. 1 hr.
7/26/12	Worked on front of lower cowl with epoxy. 2 hrs.
7/27/12	Continued to shape front of lower cowl with epoxy. 4 hrs.
7/28/12	More adjustments and fitting of spinner. 3 hrs.
7/29/12	Final fitting and installing of nut plates on fore spinner backer plate. 3 hrs.
7/30/12	Fabricated and cut out cowling and glassed decorative cover for side cowl hinge wire. 3 hrs.
7/31/12	Jason Moorefield came to the shop. Added extra wire for transponder. Answered questions and showed me how to hook up the engine sensor wires to the D-sub male and female connectors. 2 hrs.
8/1/12	Installed nut plates to hold decorative covers for side cowl hinges. 1 hr.
8/2/12	Installed aluminum heat shield on entire interior side of lower cowl. Painted epoxy on entire interior side of upper cowl. Filed out notches for side cowl hinge safety wires to fit. 7 hrs.
8/4/12	Steven Brinly gave Nate his first flying lesson for an hour. CJ rode in the back seat and got some great shots of Smith Mt. Lake. After landing, CJ and Nate switched places and CJ got to fly for about 15 minutes.
8/5/12	Worked on getting the piano hinge wire to insert more easily into the left side cowling hinge. 1.5 hrs.
8/6/12	Connected engine wires to two D-sub connectors. 4.5 hrs.
8/7/12	Installed push-to-talk wires on pilot grip and stick. 1 hr.
8/8/12	Installed push-to-talk wires on co-pilot grip and stick. Painted spinner bulkheads and took old 2" pins out of prop. 2 hr.
8/9/12	Installed spinner bulkheads and spacer on prop, then installed prop on engine. Determined size of bolts, washers, and nuts for aileron pushrods and rear wing attach point and installed them temporarily. 2 hrs.
8/10/12	Reinstalled bolt and washers on throttle cable to fuel injector arm. 1 hr.

8/11/12	Installed exterior brake lines (Bonaco braided); torqued and safety-wired prop bolts. Cleaned up the shop and had 3 other couples over for dinner and plane talk. Nice evening—the weather even cooperated and wasn't too hot. 3 hrs.
8/12/12	Applied plastic tape (UHMW?) to both flaps. 1 hr.
8/18/12	Steve Scriven & Doug Barnett came to the shop today. Answered several questions and looked over the engine and the work that had been done since they were here a few months ago. Located bolts, washers, and nuts for misc. attachment point of wing to fuselage. Fabricated 4 steel parts for attaching rudder cable to rudder pedals. 3 hrs.
8/19/12	Primed and painted 4 steel rudder parts after measuring and drilling final hole positions. 2 hrs.
8/20/12	Connected the rudder pedals to the rudder cables. 1 hr.
8/21/12	Cut hole in rear baggage area bulkhead wall for the ELT indicator. Routed wire from ELT to ELT indicator. Applied the wing-walk material. 3 hrs.
8/22/12	Installed batteries and documented the same in the ELT and the ELT indicator. Then put the ELT in its holder and attached the wires. 1 hr.
8/24/12	Installed large "EXPERIMENTAL" sign on the rear baggage wall and "not built to standard procedures" plaque on the front panel. Also put a few more descriptive labels on the front panel. 3 hrs.
9/5/12	Installed new Odyssey battery. 1 hr.
9/8/12	Installed remote antenna for iFly GPS. 2 hrs.
9/9/12	Put labels on gas caps. 1 hr.
9/10/12	Flushed each tank out with 4 gallons of gas each. 1 hr.
9/13/12	Filled brake lines with fluid, cleaned canopy where it sits on the roll bar, and installed UHMW tape on the canopy where it rests on the roll bar. 4 hrs.
9/15/12	Removed canopy, caulked and sealed the seam of top fuselage where the canopy hinges are attached, prepared trailer for transporting plane, put wings on wing stands in trailer, and moved plane around in the shop so that it can be put on trailer; prepared to paint the fuselage steps. 6 hrs.
9/16/12	Ordered edge grip seal from McMaster Carr. PN 1120A711. For front edge of canopy, to be installed on the fuselage.
9/18/12	Taped off, sanded, and primed both steps. Finished caulking front bulkhead at fore base of canopy. 2 hrs.
9/19/12	Taped off, washed, and Scotch-brited front part of fuselage immediately behind the firewall. 2 hrs.

9/20/12	Finished taping everything off and covering the plane. Used mineral spirits to wipe off the part being painted. Primed the front top part of the fuselage. 3 hrs.
9/22/12	Compounded and polished the 2 trim strips between wing root and fuselage. 2 hrs.
9/23/12	Steve Harsh came to my shop and applied the finish coat and the clear coat on the steps and the front top fuselage areas that were painted.
9/24/12	Ken Moore helped me reinstall the canopy after I put the weather-stripping on the front fuselage where the canopy meets the fuselage. Didn't fit right. Still fooling with it. 2 hrs.
9/25/12	Went with a narrower weather-stripping and it worked well. Figured out how to load plane into the BecoBall trailer and then secure the ramp for travel. 2 hrs.
9/28/12	Finished cutting 8 large trees in the front yard and cleaning up a very large mess. Jarett Wilkes was the tree cutter. Dad arrived around 5 p.m. and helped with the last of the cleanup. Tomorrow we go to the hangar.
9/29/12	Moving Day! Dad, CJ, Steven Brinly, Bill Bowen, and Bob Williams all helped to transport and unload the fuselage and wings and then install the wings. A very good day except for the prop rubbing the top of the trailer door and putting some light scratches in the prop. 6 hrs.

"Accomplishment" and "success" and "victory" and "achievement" were all words that jumped into my mind as I towed my big box trailer to the hangar with a plane sticking out the back. Pride was also right there in the mix as I watched people do a double take. I was actually taking my airplane—hitherto land-bound—to the place where planes fly. The wings went on quickly with the help of all those extra hands, and the plane soon looked as though she belonged at an airport.

10/2/12	Worked on getting nuts on wing bolts. 2 hrs.
10/3/12	Used rivet gun to drive in two stubborn wing bolts and put a few more nuts on. 2 hrs.
10/4/12	Used a pry bar to back out one bolt that was in too far. Put the last nut on and then tightened the nuts. Had to grind down a 5/8" open wrench in order to get it on the nut. 3 hrs.

Imagine seeing this going down the highway.

Hangar assembly crew. Left to right:
Bob Williams, Charlie Hagerty, Bill Bowen, me,
CJ Hagerty, and Steven Brinly.

10/6/12	Pam & Scott Trask flew down from Upper Michigan this weekend. Scott and I flew in his 7A today for about one hour. Very windy. Scott did the landings.
10/16/12	Finally back to work after spending the last several days cutting down several large trees in the front yard, cleaning up, restoring the yard with 4 tandem loads of dirt, and then reseeding everything. Connected everything at the wing roots such as the fuel line, fuel vent line, and electrical connections. 2 hrs.
10/17/12	Installed wing tips; started permanently connecting the ailerons and flaps. 4 hrs.
10/18/12	Ailerons are off a bit. Spent last night looking at forums and also called Van's yesterday. Took my bell crank jig and rechecked ailerons. Steven Brinly came over to hangar and offered an idea. Labeled fuel selector with temporary labels. Applied N number decals and tempus fugit decals. Checked straightness of prop. 6 hrs.
10/19/12	Readjusted the control stick to pushrod joint in order to get the stick vertical. Installed bell crank jig and removed left wing tip in order to work out the aileron problem. 2 hrs.
10/20/12	Spent all day adjusting the ailerons and flaps. Everything seems to be right on the money, except now the left wing tip is about 16/32s higher than the left aileron when in the neutral position. 7 hrs.
10/23/12	Applied NO STEP (2) and NO PUSH (6) decals. Riveted plate nuts (4) onto center floor fuselage console to mount fire extinguisher holder. 2 hrs.
10/24/12	Labeled fuel selector permanently. 1 hr.
10/30/12	Installed misc. panels on interior for purposes of weight and balance. 1 hr.
11/1/12	Picked up painted cowling, spinner and fuselage to vertical stabilizer fairing from my painter Steve Harsh. Also, put in 8 quarts of oil. 1 hr.
11/3/12	Had lunch at hangar. CJ, Megan, and Nathan all stopped by to help pick the color of the interior seats. Ordered these from Abby at Frontline Interiors. CJ was the best help on colors. Installed the front cowling and spinner. 2 hrs.
11/5/12	Steven Brinly brought scales to the hangar and we weighed the plane [and] then did the weight and balance configurations. 2 hrs.
11/15/12	Brooks Smith inspected the plane and issued certificate of airworthiness, and Manuel Cervalho issued repairman's certificate. 2 hrs.

Dad helping me put the wing bolts in.

This is the point at which the FAA comes to visit, and—if everything meets their approval—declares that your homebuilt contraption is now (a) officially christened and (b) acknowledged as a genuine flying machine. This legal blessing, with its accompanying piece of paper, is called a "certificate of airworthiness."

Another official piece of paper that you try to get at this time is a repairman's certificate. If you've kept good records and can show that you did indeed build at least 51 percent of your plane, this coveted document will allow you to do your own repair work and annual inspections. You can't work on any other planes, but you can work on this one plane. This was almost as exciting as getting married, and yes, I did get pictures.

Proudly holding my certificate of airworthiness, with DAR Brooks Smith (left) and FAA representative Manuel Cervalho posing for this momentous occasion.

11/17/12	Reinstalled 6 inspection plates on wing bottoms after rechecking all connections and applying torque seal on a couple of nuts. Installed 2 adel clamps on each wing root fuel line. Installed spinner. Started to install wing root fairings. 4 hrs.
11/18/12	Worked on pumping fuel with the electric fuel pump. Right tank picked up, but left tank did not. Still trying. 3 hrs. 20 gallons, $113.00.
11/20/12	Found the problem: Loose AN fittings at the wing root. Tightened these up and it pumped fuel right away. Put the right wing root fairing partially on. 1 hr.
11/23/12	Checked one more time for any fuel leaks and then finished installing the wing root fairing. 1 hr.
11/24/12	Checked operation of ELT and then installed rear baggage wall pieces. Got most of the fuselage inspection covers on after double-checking all visible nuts and bolts. 5 hrs.
11/28/12	Installed and blind-riveted the two fuselage vertical side cover plates. 2 hrs.

11/29/12	Flew 1.4 hrs. with Steven Brinly in a 172. Fixed a loose Molex connector for right strobe. 1 hr.
12/1/12	Flew 1.5 hrs. with Steven Brinly in a 172. Installed baggage side wall covers and fuel valve and fuel pump covers. 2 hrs.
12/3/12	Installed door latch spring. 1 hr.
12/4/12	Seats arrived from Flightline Interiors a few days ago. Installed them, adjusted seat back position, and adjusted seat belts. 2 hr.
12/5/12	Tried to fly with Steven today, but we had an alternator problem and had to taxi back to the hangar. Tested the ELT.
12/6/12	Flew 1.1 hrs. with Steven Brinly in a 172. All pattern work. Pretty busy.
12/7/12	Tried to fly today, but the ceiling was too low.
12/8/12	Installed floor pans. Still looking at EFIS/EMS. 2 hrs.
12/11/12	Flew 1.2 hrs with Steven. 11 touch and gos.
12/13/12	Flew 1.3 hrs. with Steven.
12/14/12	Talked with TruTrak and determined that my 25-pin D-subs are backwards. That's why my EMS is not working. 1 hr.

Wiring my engine monitoring system (EMS) backwards was probably the biggest mistake I made on the entire project. It wasn't an expensive mistake—new 25-pin D-subs cost less than $30.00—but what a pain! It was tedious enough when I first wired those two fancy wire connectors together in the shop, where it was warm and I was working on a bench with good light. Now I had to do it all over again in a cold hangar while standing and reaching up to the back of the engine in a tight space. My back hurt for three days.

12/15/12	Bought a new male and female 25-pin D-sub connector. Rewired both connectors. EMS now works. 5 hrs.
12/18/12	I've been studying FARs and AIMs. Flew 0.9 hrs. with Steven in very windy conditions. Did 6 crosswind landings and takeoffs. Got signed off for Biennial Flight Review.
12/19/12	Still programming EMS. 2 hrs.
12/20/12	Doug, Steve, and Dave LaPrade all went with me to see Hatcher Ferguson's plane. I also talked with Ricky Franklin, the CFI and test pilot.
12/27/12	Installed top spark plugs. Reattached 37-pin D-sub connectors between the EDM and the EFIS and resecured the wires. 3 hrs.
12/28/12	Installed front fuselage carpet on floor. 2 hrs.
12/29/12	Rigged up heater to bring the oil temp up before trying to start engine. 1 hr.

1/1/13	Started the engine for the first time! Gary & Joan Wooldridge, Ed Davis, CJ, Megan, and Gail were all there to help. Started the engine for the second time and then taxied about 100 yards.

There were so many high-water marks and big accomplishments throughout the whole process that I would be hard-pressed to pick a favorite. But if I had to pick something—other than the first flight—it would have to be starting the engine for the first time. Combining so many inanimate parts into a beautiful, roaring source of power—seemingly alive—literally had me shaking with excitement.

Getting ready to fire this baby up with Gary Wooldridge, CJ Hagerty, and Ed Davis providing extra sets of eyes.

1/5/13	Went to Roanoke to fly Hatcher Ferguson's plane. Met Ricky Franklin the CFI and flew five hours.
1/6/13	Started plane and tried to adjust idle. Steve Brinly showed me how to adjust both idle and richness. Flooded plane and drained battery.
1/7/13	Returned to try to start plane. Would not start.
1/8/13	Checked for fuel leaks. Found that the fuel valve was labeled incorrectly. Relabeled fuel valve, checked fuel flow, and started engine. Ricky Franklin and Glenn came over to look over plane for first flight. Four small squawks. 4 hrs.
1/9/13	Replaced AN 823-8D fitting for the oil cooler line because of a drip. 4 hrs.

1/10/13	Final adjustment on idle and richness. Did a moderate-speed taxi on runway 17. Looked over engine again. Installed lower cowl. 4 hrs.
1/11/13	Trimmed empennage fairing where elevator rods were rubbing. Trimmed opening in bottom of fuselage where flap rods were rubbing. Finished installing lower cowl. Installed upper cowl. 4 hrs.
	1,816 hours of total construction time.
1/12/13	Washed and dried plane. Nathan and Alex came and sat in it. Taxi with Nathan.
1/18/13	Yesterday we got about 4 inches of snow at the airport, and for the four days before that it rained steadily all day. But today was bright and sunny with a 5-mph wind, and *Ricky Franklin flew N954CH for the first time.* Twenty minutes between 2:00 and 2:30. Pulled the top cowl and checked everything. Then flew again for thirty minutes between 4:30 and 5:00. Everything seemed to work well. Oil temperature did not get quite high enough (around 155 °F), and the transponder would not signal Mode C. Easy to fix.

Gary Wooldridge brought his own personal tow motor.

The calm paragraph written above belies the real emotions I was experiencing. I'm by nature outwardly unemotional, and I probably didn't act all that excited on that 18th day of January. But trust me—I was more than just excited! It was thrilling beyond words to see something I had built with my own hands actually flying. The white of the snow on the ground, the crystal-clear blue of the sky, and the polished shine of my plane cutting smoothly through the air was everything I had thought it would be, and more. I'll never forget that day. Seeing my wife in her wedding dress and being in the delivery room when both my sons were born were the only things I could think of that would top that experience. I can't adequately describe it even now.

You'll notice that on 11/29/12 I flew with Steven Brinly for the first time in a long time, beginning the final stage of this lengthy homebuilding process. I now owned a working airplane, and I needed to sharpen my dormant piloting skills because in just a few short weeks I would be entrusting my life to the machine that had slowly taken shape in my shop.

Five

You Know It's a Bad Landing When...

EXCEPT FOR TEN SHORT FLIGHTS OVER THE LAST TWENTY-NINE years, I had not done any real "pilot-in-command" flying since June 1979, and I guess you could say I was rusty (I guess you could also say the Burj Khalifa in Dubai is a tall building). I needed to begin studying and flying again in order to attain the competency level required to safely operate my new plane. An RV-7A is a fully aerobatic 200-mph plane. It's light and responsive, and although it's not considered to be a high-performance plane—it doesn't have retractable gear and over 200 horsepower—it is definitely not a trainer. Some describe the 7A as "twitchy," while others say it's responsive. One thing for certain, it wasn't going to handle like any of the Cessnas or Pipers I'd flown before.

Like every other venture in life, you've got to crawl before you walk, and fortunately Steven Brinly was there to help with the process of crawling. Steven had already played a big part in the final construction of the plane, and now he was going to assist in the preparation of the pilot. Anyone who has taken flying lessons knows that the personality of your instructor is a key factor in your success: "Taciturn" and "misanthropic" are not words you want to associate with a CFI. Steven and I got along great.

I had told Steven the limited history of my flying experiences, and in late November 2012—as I was putting the finishing touches on my plane (then at the hangar)—we took off in a Cessna 172 from Lynchburg Regional Airport. I'd been doing several things to prepare for this re-entry into the world of aviation, including listening to the tower. Lynchburg is a controlled airport, and if you are in their airspace you don't do anything without first talking to a controller. I won't say it went well the first time, but I had been doing a lot of listening on the radio and was able to at least understand most of what was being said.

That first flight was uneventful. I got reacquainted with the area—everything looks different from the air—and I did some stalls and some slow flight before returning to the airport for a few takeoffs and landings. (Slow flight is when you ascend to a safe altitude and then slow the plane down to the minimum controllable airspeed. It's a good exercise and makes you focus on smoothly coordinating all your inputs to the plane.)

Steven and I flew six times late that year, and by the second or third time up, I was starting to feel comfortable. We worked especially on takeoffs, landings, and slow flight. On our last session together, we had a strong crosswind blowing over the runway. Steven said that if I could take off and land several times in that wind, he would approve my biennial flight review and my pilot's license would be current for the next two years. The wind was definitely a challenge, but everything went well. We bounced around for about an hour doing touch-and-gos, and then Steven signed my logbook. After 7.4 hours of instructional flying time, I was a current, legal pilot for the first time in thirty-two years!

This alone would have been exciting stuff, but more needed to be done. Just a month later—January 2013—my plane would take its maiden flight at the hands of a test pilot. Shortly after that I would fly it myself for the first time, and I wasn't ready for that yet.

Every pilot—even an experienced one—is supposed to get some "in type" training when he ventures out to fly a plane he's never flown before. It just makes good sense. The controls are essentially the same in all planes, but the handling characteristics are different.

My RV-7A was not going to handle like the C-172 I'd just finished flying with Steven, or the Piper 140 I originally learned to fly back in 1976.

To begin with, the RV has a stick, not a yoke, like the Cessna and the Piper. A yoke comes out the front panel of the plane (kind of like a steering wheel in a car), and a stick comes up out of the floor. I had only flown one other plane before with a stick, and that was the Vans RV-7A demonstrator at Sun 'n Fun ten years ago. Operating the stick was intuitive, but mastering it would take some practice—my brief time in the demonstrator showed me that. Very little stick movement was needed to make the plane quickly change directions. In both the Cessna and the Piper the yoke has to be moved a lot to get the plane to respond, but in the RV, practically all I had to do was *think* about changing direction.

Another thing that makes the RV so quick is the size of the engine as it relates to the weight of the plane. My RV has a 180-HP engine, and the empty weight of the plane is 1,055 pounds. A Cessna 172 has a 180-HP engine, but the empty weight of the plane is usually between 1,600 and 1,700 pounds. That's a big difference. The RV accelerates quicker, climbs faster, cruises faster, and is capable of doing loops and rolls. Cessnas are great planes, but they feel like lumbering trucks in comparison. I don't say that to belittle Cessnas—they've been around forever and set a high standard—but to point out that the two planes are quite different.

Here's my favorite example: When taking off in the Cessna, you push the throttle all the way open quickly and then add in the right rudder to keep the plane straight as it gradually accelerates down the runway. When I tried that same procedure on my first takeoff in the RV, I could barely keep it on the runway. Too much power! The plane accelerated faster than I expected, and it almost pulled me off the left side of the runway because I wasn't adding enough right rudder—didn't see that coming. Next time I eased the throttle open slowly, coordinated the rudder smoothly, and didn't have any trouble keeping the plane straight. *Much better.*

In order to gain some in-type training and a better feel for how my RV was going to fly, I contacted a guy in our local EAA chapter named Hatcher Ferguson. Hatcher was flying an RV-7A, just like mine, that he had built himself. Well, almost like mine; his plane had a constant speed propeller, and of course his instrument panel was laid out differently, but the body of the plane was the same, and the aircraft would handle much the way mine would.

I had met Hatcher a few times before at EAA meetings but didn't know him well. I did, however, know two other guys, Steve and Doug, who had introduced me to the first homebuilt plane I'd ever seen, and they had been friends with Hatcher for a long time. They said Hatcher would probably be willing to let me fly his plane—not by myself, of course, but with another RV-4 owner who was a good friend of Hatcher's and who was also a CFI. This guy, Ricky Franklin, had not only flown Hatcher's plane many times but also kept his own RV in the hangar on Hatcher's grass strip.

With a few phone calls the connections were made, and two weeks after I had become a current pilot again, I met Hatcher and Ricky at Hatcher's airstrip. Did I mention that Hatcher's in the dairy business? He has a barn and a large herd of cows on one side of the hill, near his house, and an airstrip on the other side of the hill—a pretty nice setup.

We met on a Saturday morning when the weather was supposed to be good all day. Hatcher took me up first for about half an hour, and when we returned to the farm Ricky was waiting. Our plan was to spend the rest of the day flying to several small airports in North Carolina. That would provide me with plenty of time to get a feel for how the plane would handle—and to practice a lot of takeoffs and landings. *This will be a good day.*

Two weeks after those RV training flights, my plane was ready, the big day was at hand, and Ricky flew her for the very first time. I wanted to do the first flight myself, but knew I wasn't the right pilot for the job. Ricky had thousands of hours of flying time, and many of those hours had been in RV planes. He'd even test-flown a few different RVs for other homebuilders. He would know if my plane was flying correctly, and he would also be better prepared to handle any possible emergency. As exciting as this moment was, discretion was still the better part of valor.

My turn would come eleven days later, when, after 1,816 hours of construction time, N954CH and I got to take our first ride in the sky. The manufacturer of Van's RV kit planes talks about having "the RV grin" the first time you fly one of their planes. They're not kidding. What a rush—I don't think I stopped smiling for the next two days.

The FAA requires most new experimental planes to stay within a designated area for their first forty hours of flight time. This is called "phase one," and it gives the pilot a chance to test a number of things on the aircraft. Paul Dye, editor-in-chief of *Kitplanes* magazine and a retired lead flight director for NASA's Human Space Flight Program, is also a consultant for flight-testing projects. He wrote a great article in the February 2013 issue of *Kitplanes* that dealt with phase-one flight testing. He likes to break this type of testing down into six different categories: engine break-in; performance testing; envelope expansion; stability and control; aerobatics and maneuvering; and avionics testing.

Paul's article was as good as any I'd seen, and it came out just as I was beginning my phase-one testing. Needless to say, I followed his advice as closely as I could. His piloting abilities are far beyond mine, but the general principles he provided were helpful even for a novice pilot like me.

Those forty hours of testing were generally uneventful. The engine ran flawlessly, and the plane flew just as well as the designer said it would. Other than two minor "squawks"—issues with the transponder and the autopilot—the only other concern was with the front baffle air dams, which I later cut down about half an inch. This helped to bring all the cylinder head temperatures into more equal alignment. I checked everything under the cowling regularly, and I changed the oil and oil filter after twenty-five hours of flying time, but that was about it. New engines are broken in using mineral oil, and after twenty-five hours you're supposed to switch to regular oil. I also changed the fuel filter at the same time, just in case there was anything hidden in the two new fuel tanks that could clog the filter and cause a problem.

Except for that first takeoff where I applied the throttle too fast, learning to handle the plane went smoothly. Applying forty degrees of flaps worked well to slow the plane down on final approach, and I made sure for the first fifteen or twenty hours that I only flew on calm days. Fortunately, I had a large area in which to fly for those first forty hours—the FAA designates the flying area for a new experimental plane when they issue the certificate of airworthiness. The first several hours were spent flying fast and running the new engine at a high rpm in order to break it in properly. After doing the engine break-in, I spent a lot of time doing takeoffs and landings and trying to follow Paul's outline—except for aerobatics, which I'm not qualified for. I did a total of 163 landings as part of phase-one testing.

After the forty-hour requirement is met—and providing that everything is working properly—you move on to phase two. In this phase there is no limit on your flying area, and passengers are permitted. The two people I took up first were Ricky Franklin and Steven Brinly; both are CFIs, and their presence in the cockpit was beneficial in several ways. For one thing, it's nice to have someone else fly the plane while you check something that requires you to keep your head down for a few minutes.

The next person I took for a ride, after Ricky and Steven, was Gail. Steven and I had just flown to Raleigh–Durham on a Saturday, and the next day Gail and I flew to a small airport just outside Raleigh. Our son Nathan and his wife Alex live in the Triangle area, and this smaller airport happened to be almost as close to their home as the large Raleigh–Durham airport. That suited me perfectly, because even though my trip with Steven had given me more confidence about flying into larger airports, I still wanted to do a few more trips with his help before I ventured out on my own to one of those big commercial hubs.

So on Sunday, we—Gail, Nathan, Alex, and I—were able to have lunch together in North Carolina. This is what I had been building for all those years: A three-hour car ride had just been reduced to a forty-minute flight. Seeing family on a regular basis was now easier. Along with Nate and Alex in North Carolina, we also had my parents—along with my brother Dan and his family—in Pennsylvania, Gail's sister and family in Wisconsin (yes, we see them every year at Oshkosh), and other relatives in Michigan, South Carolina, and

Florida. (My brother Rob and his family live in Santiago, Chile, but that's not a flight I'll be making any time soon!)

Almost three weeks after our short flight to North Carolina, Nathan had to come up to Virginia to meet with some tenants who were moving into a townhouse that he rented out. He was anxious to fly in the new plane, so we made plans to head to the airport early Saturday morning.

The day was perfect, with blue skies and calm air. By 9:00 a.m. the plane was out of the hangar, the pre-flight was complete, and Nate had been given specific instructions. (There are particular parts of the plane—such as the canopy—that you don't want to grab onto or lean against. It's also important not to step on the flaps. There is also an easy way and a hard way to lower yourself into the seat, and one or two parts that you don't want to bump on the way down.) I was obviously aware of all these things, but I knew that everyone who got in for the first time would need to be cautioned. *Who am I kidding? I'm going to tell everyone to be careful every time they get in.*

In a minute or two we were both seated, and I showed Nate how to secure the Hooker harness and lap belt. We also talked about what I would be doing, where he needed to keep his feet and his hands, and how we would be maintaining a "sterile cockpit." He had flown a few times before in Cessna 172s, and had even taken his own first instructional flight several months earlier, but this would be the first time he was going to fly with just me. I'm sure he was nervous but he

Just about ready to take Nate up for his first ride.

didn't show it, and it looked like I had a "ready and willing passenger."

Everything went well. We had a smooth takeoff and then took a beautiful one-hour scenic tour over the gorgeous Blue Ridge Mountains. Part of the time was spent demonstrating the Garmin Aera 510 GPS and the iFly 700 GPS that are mounted in the plane's panel. They're both nice pieces of equipment and make navigating much safer and easier. Nate did the flying about half the time and did a good job of maintaining both altitude and heading, but he's never done a landing by himself, so he gave the plane back to me as we returned to the airport. The winds were still calm and the landing was just the way I like it—routine.

What a great time! Nathan had a first-rate "RV grin," and we took several good pictures of him with the plane. After that he had to go to his appointment, and then he would be driving south to meet his wife at the beach in North Carolina. We hugged and said good-bye, and I pointed out that he'd be much safer traveling back home if he were flying.

He would remind me of those words later on.

—

Right after he left I called Gail, to let her know we were down safely and that Nate was heading back home. She suggested that since the day was so nice, we should fly up to Pennsylvania to visit my parents. We had tried to do that trip the weekend before, but low clouds had caused us to turn around when we were only about ten minutes out of Lynchburg. Tomorrow would be Father's Day, so I agreed, and proceeded to refuel the plane. I also looked over the destination airport diagram, programmed the radio frequencies, set the GPS units, took note of airports along the way, and called 1-800-WXBRIEF to make sure the weather was going to remain good for the rest of the day.

Gail arrived at the airport around 11:30, and by 11:50 we were strapped in and feeling the rush of heading down runway 10. In just a few minutes we were at 4,500 feet and headed north. The wind had picked up a little since the morning, but it was still a much calmer trip than our flight to North Carolina had been a few weeks ago. We were both having a good time—the view over the Appalachian Mountains was stunning, and Gail kept busy taking pictures and spotting landmarks.

A good look at the Appalachian Mountains.

I'd been living in Virginia for thirty-eight years and had made the drive between Virginia and Pennsylvania more times than I could remember. It was a five-and-a-half-hour scenic trip that I didn't mind, but to be able to make the same trip in one-and-a-half hours, above panoramas like this, was more than just fun…it was exhilarating! Flying, to me, is a great combination of both the practical (speed) and the poetic (scenery). I love shadows on mountains, sunlight glinting off ponds, small towns nestled into valleys, isolated homesteads on mountain tops, small looping rural roads, changing colors in the sky, and the melding of all this as the view stretches to the horizon.

But at the same time, I was also concentrating on the task at hand—flying the plane. This was the longest cross-country trip I'd ever taken, as the sole pilot, in any small plane. In fact, that trip down to North Carolina three weeks previously had been the first time I had flown out of Virginia without one of my CFI friends. Heading south out of Lynchburg is actually much easier than flying north, simply because the ground is flat. Now, as we headed for Pennsylvania, I was intensely aware of just how high and rugged the Appalachians are. There were also broken clouds along the way that I needed to avoid. Between maintaining the right altitude (above the mountains, but below the clouds), watching for other planes, following landmarks on the ground, finding potential emergency landing areas, monitoring the instrument panel, and navigating the proper heading, I was busy doing a lot more than just enjoying the view.

Ten miles away from the destination airport (KAOO), I announced on the radio our location and our intention to land. There was no other traffic in the area at the time except for one other pilot who was preparing to take off. He said he would be taking off on runway 3. Now, when preparing to land, even at a familiar airport, you would normally fly over the airport to get a look at the wind sock and observe both the direction and the approximate speed of the wind. This time, because this other pilot was on the ground getting ready to depart, I simply talked with him and verified that the winds were indeed favorable for runway 3. Our northerly heading had us lined up already with 3 for a straight-in final approach, and since there were no other planes in the sky or on the ground, that's what I announced we would do. The wind was gusting toward us around 10 or 12 knots from an angle of about 1 or 2 o'clock, but we were doing fine—lined up and on speed. The runway was 100 feet wide and over 5,900 feet long, so compared with what I was used to at my home airport, this landing should be simple. Maybe that thought caused me to relax a second too soon.

The time was 1:15 p.m., and puffy white clouds still dotted the blue sky. We were bouncing around a little as we descended, but I'd landed many times in stronger winds. The runway threshold flashed below us, flaps were forty degrees down, airspeed was bleeding off nicely, and my flare was at the right height above the ground. Then the main wheels touched the asphalt, and suddenly everything went very wrong! The mains were on the ground for just a second, and *boom,* we were back up in the air. I bounced the landing, and it happened so fast I didn't react. Did a combination of ground effect and gusting wind create enough lift to bring the plane back up? Was my flare really at the right height? Did I lose focus at the wrong instant?

Whatever the reason, we came down hard, and the front nose wheel buckled with a terrible scraping sound. Immediately I thought of fire. The bent wheel was pulling us hard to the left and off the runway. There was a split second to pull the mixture control back and shut the engine down just before we hit the soft dirt and flipped. Instantly there was a crushing sensation in my neck as my head was driven into the ground with the weight of the plane on top of me.

PART

II

Even our misfortunes are a part of our belongings.

— Antoine de Saint-Exupéry, *Night Flight*

Six

Emergency 911

EVERYTHING WAS BLACK—I MUST HAVE CLOSED MY EYES WHEN WE left the runway—and I realized that the impact had raised the plane up on its nose and flipped it over, smashing the canopy, and trapping us both upside down in our seats. Panic, shock, and adrenaline all kicked in, and my mind raced. *Is Gail all right? Why can't I move my right hand? We're trapped in the plane! Gail, I'm so sorry! We've got to get out of here before it catches fire! Is anybody coming to help?* These and a hundred other thoughts whirled through my head as we hung by our shoulder harnesses and lap belts.

Gail opened her eyes and said she wasn't hurt badly, but she was wedged in and couldn't move. There's not much extra room between the bottom of the seat and the top of the plane's canopy. Gail's a few inches taller than I am, so I could move a little, but she was jammed between the ground and the seat.

Fortunately the accident shattered the Plexiglas canopy. I struggled to untangle myself from the seat cushions around me, and then had the presence of mind to pull at the pieces of broken canopy, trying to make a large enough hole to get out. This hard Plexiglas material was broken into small-to-medium-sized pieces—and luckily some of them were missing—but progress was slow because I could only use my left hand. Mercifully, after several minutes, I had some help: an airport employee who pulled up in a golf cart. I learned later that he was the only person working at the time. He jumped out and scrambled under the wing to help me dislodge some of the broken pieces. He was a God-send, and a couple of weeks after the accident I learned his name and called to thank him.

Just when the hole was big enough to crawl through, we heard ambulance sirens, and my Good Samaritan had to go unlock the gate so the ambulance could get through. He assured me he'd be right back. After he left, I was able to lower myself completely onto the ground and slowly slide on my back through the hole. I then reached back through the hole with my left hand to help free Gail. My right hand was useless. Oddly, except during the initial impact, I wasn't aware of much pain in my neck. If anyone had known then how badly my neck was broken—and where it was broken—they would have had me on a backboard and in a neck brace immediately. Instead I just kept working, fearful that the plane would erupt in flames.

The white stuff all around the plane is fire-retardant foam that the firemen put down.

The first thing I had to do for Gail was try to free her arms so that she could start to help herself. Her torso was twisted, and her right shoulder was resting on the ground. The headset and its cord were tangled around her, and her seat cushions were pinning her arms to her side; her position could have easily caused panic and claustrophobia, but she remained calm. Once she could move her arms she released the buckle on the lap and harness belts and eased her back onto the ground. From this position she was able to slide on her back through the hole in the canopy and free herself from the plane. Little bugs jumped on us as we lay together, dazed, on the damp grass. Neither of us was bleeding much; Gail had a few small cuts on her face, and I had a small gash on my right shin.

If you look carefully, you can see the hole in the canopy that Gail and I slid through.

It may seem like a strange thing to do, but while we were both lying there, I called my brother Dan, who had been waiting for us at the airport. One of my first thoughts, as we were skidding off the runway, had been, "I hope my parents don't see this mess." Now I needed to find out how they were doing and let them know we were okay. I remember talking to Dan, but I don't remember what was said—he would tell me later.

The conversation was brief because the sirens were getting loud and the emergency vehicles were coming through the gate—two ambulances and three fire trucks. Our rescuers had arrived.

—

My two EMTs were Beth and Chad; Gail's were Ray and Rick. All four went right to work and seemed to know exactly what they were doing. They looked at the upside-down plane, and the first question they asked was whether we had any neck pain. We both answered with a very clear "yes"—and out came the neck braces. These state-of-the-art wonders of plastic, Velcro straps, and padding would become our close friends. They are restrictive, just as they're supposed to be, and when Beth first put the thing on me, I didn't like it! Little did I know what would be immobilizing my neck and head in a few days.

Beth did most of the talking as they worked over me; I'm not sure who was heading up Gail's care. She spoke calmly. I can vaguely remember her face—I think she had short blonde hair—but I can still clearly hear her voice. She asked where we were from and why we had flown here. When I told her that we had flown up to take my parents to dinner for Father's Day, she even suggested a restaurant. "If we called now, we probably wouldn't have any trouble getting a reservation," she said. In my confused state I remember hoping I could recall the name of the place so I could tell my brother about it. *Maybe I'm not too badly hurt after all if this nice girl thinks I'll still be going out for dinner tonight. I broke my right wrist once in eighth grade and learned to eat with my left hand—this shouldn't be any problem.*

Once the cervical collars were on, we were placed on the backboards and our heads were strapped down. Gail and I had been lying beside each other during the assessments, but now we were lifted up onto gurneys and placed into separate ambulances. We'd been talking—I told her I was fine except for my right hand; she said she had some pain in her chest and her shoulder. I said I was sorry at least twenty times. Now she was taken away and I couldn't see her.

At some point—whether it was beside the wrecked plane, or driving through the gate of the airport—my brother's wife, Gloria, looked in through the back door of my ambulance and said that everyone would be there when we got to the hospital. I also remember somebody asking which hospital to use: There was a small medical facility in the nearby town of Martinsville and a much larger hospital further away in Altoona. Maybe they weren't even asking me and I just overheard all this. I don't know, but I'm thankful we ended up in Altoona—the smaller facility wouldn't have been able to help us.

This was my first ride in an ambulance, and trust me, they aren't designed for comfort. The padding on the gurney is hard, and the vehicle suspension is heavy-duty and stiff—think dump truck. You feel each bump in the road, and by this time the adrenaline was wearing off and the pain in my neck was increasing with every mile. The ride to the hospital took almost thirty minutes, and I closed my eyes in an effort to block out the reality of what was happening. Gail has always been prone to motion sickness, and it was worse for her in the other ambulance.

The enormity of our situation was starting to register. I was hurt, possibly badly; Gail was hurt, and it was probably worse than she thought; our family would be worried and upset; and I had business appointments next week. *How much will this end up costing after insurance? What if there's nerve damage to my hand and it never works again? How would the accident disrupt family members' schedules?* And finally, I could hardly bear to think about what had just happened to the beautiful plane I had carefully worked on for so long.

As the ambulance pulled in beside the emergency room doors, my niece Wanda was there waiting. She hadn't been at the airport, but her father, my brother Dan, had called her. He had to stay behind at the airport to talk with the state police when they arrived, and he wanted to make sure that someone was at the hospital to meet us. Dan knows hospitals, and he has strong feelings about never going to one by yourself. My parents were driving there in their own car, but he knew the ambulances would arrive much faster than they would.

We were wheeled from the ambulances to separate emergency rooms. I kept asking the medical personnel how Gail was, and she kept asking them how I was. Both of us were in pain, but nothing could be done for that until the extent of our injuries had been determined. The next three to four hours became a rotation of rolling beds, CT scans, x-rays, MRIs, and painful transfers from bed to table and back again. First Gail would be rolled down a hallway, and then half an hour later she'd be back and I'd be rolled down the same hall. By now several family members, and even some friends, were at the ER and talking with us. The one advantage of not yet being on pain medication was that we were at least able to converse somewhat coherently. I remember making a phone call to my answering service and telling them to cancel everything that I had on the books—I was beginning to realize I had a long-term problem. *I'll bet we won't even get to go to that restaurant tonight.* As the test results started coming back, it became apparent that we wouldn't be leaving the hospital any time soon.

Oddly, I didn't call either of our sons. I had just been flying with Nathan that morning, and knew he was either at the beach by now or still driving. I thought CJ was at home in Lynchburg, but since it was such a nice Saturday there was a good chance he was on his boat fishing, up at the lake. I heard from someone that my mother had called Nathan, and I guess I assumed that someone had surely called CJ also.

The truth is, I was experiencing a lot of mixed emotions at the time, and one of them was embarrassment. Embarrassed that I had injured myself; embarrassed that I had injured my sons' mother; and embarrassed that I had wrecked my long-held obsession. Yes, it was an accident, and yes, stuff happens, but I had been talking about this plane and the greatness of flying for a long time. Suddenly it all didn't look so great. I blamed the crash on the gusting wind, but in the back of my mind was the thought that if I had been a better pilot, I would have handled things differently. My shining sense of pride in both building the plane and in learning to fly again was now badly tarnished.

It was embarrassing, too, to have become one of the NTSB's flying-related statistics. Since almost everyone has some fear of flying—some a crippling fear—I had heard lots of naysaying comments while working on my plane, starting with the less-than-tactful "Are you nuts or what?" Now, after my accident, I felt that I had solidified in many people's minds the idea that flying isn't safe—and that I was indeed crazy.

This was also the first time in my life that I had felt truly helpless. I remember later, in the ICU, that my mother asked me, "Why do you close your eyes so much?"—and I told her it was because of the pain. That was only partly true: Another factor was my acute awareness that in the hospital I had become completely reliant on others. This weakness and sense of dependency was settling heavily on me as I lay there with my neck immobilized, in pain, and unable to move. Life was out of my control, the future was uncertain, and I closed my eyes because I was trying to hide.

Emotional conflict was probably the real reason I didn't call CJ and Nate that Saturday. Nate did, however, receive a call from my mother while he was still on the road to Holden Beach. He knew what time Gail and I had departed Lynchburg, and he knew how long the trip would take. By his reckoning we should have arrived, and he was thinking about giving us a call to see how the flight had gone. Then his phone rang—Mom was crying, but she was at least able to provide the basics. Dan arrived at the emergency room a short while later and called Nate back to provide more up-to-date information. Details were still sketchy because test results weren't back yet, but I think that was a good thing, because CJ and Nate were not overly alarmed by Dan's descriptions and didn't feel as though they had to get to Altoona as fast as they could.

CJ and Megan were both in New Jersey visiting one of CJ's college friends. Both Joe and CJ had graduated from Temple University, and on that Saturday CJ, Megan, Joe, and Kim (Joe's wife) were in downtown Philadelphia at Pat's Steaks. So they were much closer to Altoona when Dan called than if they had been home in Virginia. But because Dan didn't want to alarm them—and because nobody knew the full extent of our injuries yet—he didn't convey a sense of urgency. He said that although the plane had flipped, we appeared to be just scraped up and would probably be okay. CJ called Dan later that night to see how we were doing, but the information available still hadn't changed much. So the next afternoon (Sunday), CJ and Megan drove from Philly to Altoona. By then the seriousness of the injuries had been determined, and they were more than a little shocked to see me in the ICU.

Back on her landing gear and being towed to the hangar.

It only took a day or two for the FAA, the NTSB, my insurance adjuster, and the Altoona–Blair County Airport to get in touch. They all needed answers. We decided that since Nathan and Alex had fairly flexible schedules, they would be best able to stay with Gail and me once they arrived at the hospital. CJ and Megan could help the most by returning to Lynchburg, where my logbooks and insurance papers were kept. CJ owns an insurance agency and was the best person to talk with the insurance people and handle all the paperwork. He and Megan only stayed at the hospital for four hours and then left around 8:00 p.m. for the long drive home.

Alex had been at the beach with her parents for a few days before Nate went to meet her there, and by now they knew that their vacation was going to be cut short. On Sunday morning, the day after the accident, they left Holden Beach and drove first to their home in Durham to pick up some things they would need. Next, they drove to Alex's parents' home in Haw River, North Carolina, where they exchanged their car for an Escalade SUV—the perfect vehicle to transport me home with, if needed. Oh, how I wish we had decided to use that vehicle!—but I'll get to that later on. Then they continued on to our home in Goode, Virginia, to pick up clothes and personal effects for Gail and me; we hadn't packed anything, of course, because we weren't intending to be away overnight. Finally they began the five-and-a-half-hour drive to the hospital in Altoona, where they arrived around 11:00 p.m. That Sunday was a long and stressful one for them.

Gail had been discharged from the hospital earlier that same Sunday, but she stayed with Mom, Dad, and Dan at the hospital all afternoon, talking with CJ and Megan. When CJ and Megan left to return to Virginia, everyone else stayed in my room as we waited for Nate and Alex to arrive that evening. Unless you're a medical professional, it's always shocking to see someone hooked up in an intensive care unit—it was especially hard on my parents—but I was glad everyone had been able to come. As it worked out, Nate and Alex both cleared their schedules and were available to help us for two weeks, until June 29. We talked briefly about what CJ and Nate would need to do the next day, and then, since everyone was tired, the family dispersed: Gail went home with my parents, and Nate and Alex with our friends Tim and Lisa Parnell.

And I prepared myself for a second blurry night in the ICU. Already I was beginning to learn things I had never wanted to know.

Seven

Hospitals and Halos

NOW THAT I'VE DESCRIBED WHERE OUR FAMILY WAS AND WHAT everyone had to do on both Saturday and Sunday, let me back up a bit. The number of tests done on Saturday afternoon, when Gail and I were first brought into the ER, was amazing. We each had several x-rays, two CT scans, and an MRI. The hardest part of all this testing was being moved around so much, because I was in a lot of pain by now and I wasn't supposed to strain or exert anything. The nurses and assistants had to move me from bed to table and then back to the bed; sometimes they did this job better than other times.

I don't remember having any problems when the x-rays were taken, and I didn't have any unusual difficulties during either of the CT scans, but Gail wasn't so lucky. She had to be injected with dye for one of the CT scans, and there was a "blowout" because the nurse missed her vein. Instead of going into the vein, the dye went under the skin on the back of Gail's hand and made a large subcutaneous bubble. She wasn't happy. I don't remember if I was injected with dye for either of my CT scans, but I imagine I probably was.

My problem came when staff took me to do the MRI. Even on a good day an MRI is not exactly pleasant, and this machine was not the new, open type but a very old (and noisy) model—essentially a long metal tube. The technicians lay you on your back and slide you into this long, narrow, tubular machine via a motorized table. To say it feels claustrophobic is a terrible understatement, and I could understand all over again why some people panic and have to be sedated. Fortunately—from an experience standpoint—I'd had three MRIs done years ago. On those occasions music was played through headphones, and by breathing deeply, closing my eyes, and concentrating on the music, I was able to get through the procedures. This machine, however, was like a medieval torture device, and it would require an entirely different level of endurance.

First, I was already uncomfortable and in pain before we began. Next, I also had a large neck brace on that posed a real challenge for the medical staff—they couldn't fit me and the brace in the tube. They tried, they pushed, they talked, and then they pushed some more. This went on for several minutes. At one point I had to remind them that my neck was probably broken and that maybe we should be approaching this dilemma a little more gently! I don't know what was eventually shifted or adjusted, but they finally got my head and neck brace started into the machine. The third problem was that I had too many blankets on, and once in the tube, I started to sweat—a lot. This was miserable. Whatever clothes I still had on got wet, along with my neck brace, which became itchy when it got damp. Sweat was stinging my eyes, but I couldn't raise my hands to wipe it away.

As if all of this wasn't bad enough, there was worse to come—the deafening noise. During my previous MRIs the headphones had kept out most of the noise, while simultaneously providing a nice musical distraction. Not so today. The nurses, MRI operators, inquisitors, or whatever their title, were only able to provide me with a set of foam earplugs. These might have done some good if they had been properly inserted, but as soon as the staff began the procedure, the earplugs fell out—both of them. Oh, my word, was it loud—an incredibly hard-driving, pulsating loud, like a jackhammer on steroids!

The operators told me to hold very still so they could get me out as quickly as possible, but they didn't say how long "quickly" would be. The first minute seemed to last forever. The second minute seemed four times longer. I had a call button in my left hand, and between the sweat, the pain, the itching, the stinging, the confinement, and the pounding noise that was threatening to split my skull, I really wanted to push it and get out. I suffered through another minute, then two more minutes, and then three more minutes. I counted to sixty over and over again, and thought that surely we'd be finished soon. We had to get these pictures. So I held on and concentrated on counting for twenty-three excruciating minutes. Suddenly the pounding stopped and the sliding table started to move forward out of the tube. What an *unbelievable* relief!

When they rolled me back to the ER, I told Dan that if I didn't count the plane wreck, that MRI had easily been the worst single experience of my life. And it was, but at least it had only lasted for a little over twenty minutes. Other procedures, I would discover, were going to have to be tolerated much longer.

After all the pictures had been taken and the doctors and technicians had had time to analyze them, the neurosurgeon came to my room. It was now around 8:00 p.m. on Saturday. I had been moved to the ICU and given morphine, so my recollection of the conversation is foggy. I remember being told that there were five breaks in my neck vertebrae—two breaks in C1, one in C2, one in C6, and one in C7—and that an immediate surgery to stabilize C6 and C7 was needed. I remembered what happened to the actor Christopher Reeve, who had been paralyzed after a C1 fracture, and thought, *This is starting to sound serious*. They wanted to do a permanent fusion of C6 and C7 as soon as possible; tentative plans had been made to perform the operation late on Sunday.[1]

---

[1] For a fascinating account of a similar injury, Google "On Breaking One's Neck" by Arnold Relman, M.D. Dr. Relman, then aged 90, is a professor emeritus of medicine and social medicine at Harvard Medical School and a former editor of the *New England Journal of Medicine*. He broke his neck in a fall down a staircase just twelve days after my own accident. He sustained cervical fractures that were not severe enough to require surgery,

Dr. Matt Maserati—"Just like the car," he told me—would be the primary physician overseeing my care and performing the fusion surgery. Dr. Maserati was a long way from his home town of Palo Alto, California, having completed all of his higher education on the east coast. On paper he sounded exceedingly qualified—degrees from Dartmouth and Columbia, followed by internship and residency at the University of Pittsburgh—but in person he looked awfully young. I understood that he was more than competent to wield very sharp instruments in close proximity to my spinal cord—but still…! Along with Dr. Maserati, Dr. Jim Burke would be assisting with my care. Both were with Allegheny Brain & Spine Surgeons—Maserati had joined in 2012, and Burke had been there since 2003.

Everyone agreed the fusion needed to be done quickly. Some problems developed, however, with both staffing and equipment. Apparently there was a piece of equipment that Dr. Maserati felt was best operated by a specific staff member who was not available on Sunday. Dr. Maserati was willing to proceed anyway, if that's what I wanted, but what I most wanted was for Dr. Maserati to be completely confident. If that meant we should wait an extra day, then that's what I wanted also.

By now I was resting, uncomfortably, in the ICU of the Altoona hospital and praying that everything being done for me would be done correctly. *Not my will but yours, but please don't let this get any worse.* I didn't yet have a morphine pump, but the morphine that the nurse kept injecting into my IV was working well. I'm sure I was pitiful to look at; my parents, especially my mother, had a difficult time seeing me that way. After Gail was released from the hospital Sunday afternoon, she was able to stay with me in my room. Dan was there too most of the entire weekend, and at some point on Sunday he brought me a lollipop. I said something about "morphine lollipops"—the phrase reminded me of hashish brownies—and we

---

but complications—including issues with bleeding caused by blood thinners—brought him close to death. His story is a remarkable one, and well worth reading.

both laughed. Mine was the goofy laugh of inebriation, and I think Dan was probably laughing mostly at me. It felt good, though, for a moment.

After Gail was released from the hospital, her ICU room was empty and she asked the nurses if I could be moved to that room, to create some privacy. Up to that point I had had a roommate, although there was the usual curtain between us and I don't remember anything about him. You don't get much sleep in the ICU, and this room switch may have helped a little. (Speaking of "no sleep," that ICU room on Saturday night is where I became aware of the TV show "Duck Dynasty." Someone turned the television on to A&E, and later that night there was a "Duck" marathon. Episode after episode played on, and I had no idea where the remote was. So I lay there in a drug-induced haze and watched through most of a very long night. Morphine, little sleep, and "Duck Dynasty"—what a party! By Sunday morning I was a fan.)

—

On Monday I was anxious for Dr. Maserati to do the fusion surgery. I had been in the ICU Saturday evening, all day Sunday, and Sunday night. I wasn't going to get better just lying there; the surgery was a necessity, and I was ready to get it over with. It lasted for two and a half hours, from 8:15 a.m. until 10:45, and the first challenge was the intubation.

Normally, the head is tilted back for intubation in order to establish a straighter path through a patient's airway. This wouldn't be possible in my case, however, because moving the neck could cause the broken vertebrae to shift, and damage to the spinal cord at this high cervical level could easily cause death or quadriplegia.

Installing an intubation tube is not a comfortable process even under ideal conditions, so most patients are sedated. Not me: I would have to remain conscious while the tube was being introduced, in order to demonstrate by wiggling my toes and fingers on command that my spinal cord was still intact. I also had to keep my head from moving while the tube was inserted—again, to keep the broken vertebrae from shifting. This experience was horrible—I was choking and fighting to breathe—but at least it was brief, and I either passed out or was sedated soon after they started. The sensation of having my breathing cut off, however, lasted the entire two-and-a-half-hour surgery. I vaguely remember struggling as I was coming out from under anesthesia because I was still trying to fight that feeling of being strangled.[2]

After the intubation, a horizontal incision about an inch and a half long was made in my throat to allow access to the cervical vertebrae. During the operation, the objective was to insert a piece of cadaver bone snugly between the C6 and C7 vertebrae and then immobilize those two vertebrae with a plate and some screws. Sounds simple, right? It might be if all the materials were laid out on a workbench with easy access, but Dr. Maserati would be working in a very small space through a hole in the front of my throat. He would have to be excruciatingly careful not to touch a nearby artery or the all-important spinal cord with any of the sharp instruments or screws he would be inserting into the damaged area. You've got to respect anyone who has the ability to do this type of intricate work.

After the operation, there was a drainage tube coming out of the incision, to reduce the risk of pressure from excessive fluid. I was also still wearing a large rigid neck brace because the most severe breaks—the two in C1—had not been dealt with, and my neck remained classified as "unstable." The rest of that day (and night) is a blur. I don't remember much, although I know Nathan and Alex (who had arrived the night before) were in and out of my room, along with my parents, Gail, Dan, hospital chaplains, and an assortment of other folks.

The one thing I do remember from later in the day on Monday is that Dr. Maserati came to the ICU to check on me and explain the options I had for dealing with the C1 and C2 vertebrae. The first choice was to permanently fuse these two vertebrae to the base of the skull. That area is called the occipitoatlantoaxial complex (I've been

[2] It's worth noting that when Dr. Relman needed to be intubated, the anesthesiologist was unable to do so and had to do a tracheotomy instead—and Dr. Relman's neck wasn't broken nearly as badly as mine.

waiting to use that word for months!). This surgery is a proven method of stabilizing these specific vertebrae to keep them from shifting and damaging the spinal cord. The positive side of choosing this solution is that the surgery could be done right away, and after several weeks of recovery I could start adjusting to my new state of "normal." The negative side is that I would never be able to move my head again. My neck would be rigid, and I would have to turn at the waist every time I needed to look in a different direction. I was only fifty-six, and this scenario immediately became my greatest fear.

The second choice was to attach a halo device to my head that would completely immobilize my neck and give the broken vertebrae a chance to heal. This is also a common method of dealing with broken necks, but the results could not be guaranteed. There were two breaks in C1, and one of them was very wide. Dr. Maserati believed the smaller break would almost certainly heal without any problem, but he was not very optimistic about the other, wider break. Also, I forgot to mention, these halo devices are screwed into the skull at four locations—two on the forehead and two in the back of the head—and the ungainly contraption would have to be left in place for anywhere from three to six months. What would you have done?

My lifestyle, up to this point, was not sedentary. I had to spend several hours a week working at my desk and computer, but for the most part I was pretty active. I enjoyed working in my shop, and I rode motorcycles, flew the plane, and shot rifles and handguns. I also enjoyed hiking and water sports (I earned my scuba certification years ago), and my job as a home inspector/builder kept me going up and down ladders and in and out of attics and crawl spaces. I hated the thought of giving all that up, and knew I'd have to give the halo a try. The chance of it working might be slim, but at least there *was* a chance, and I could attempt to salvage the lifestyle I was accustomed to. Dr. Maserati concurred and said he would have made the same choice for himself.

On Tuesday morning, Dr. Maserati and Dr. Burke came to my room in the ICU to install the halo. I had been given a morphine pump immediately after the surgery on Monday, and I pushed the button fervently every time I was coherent enough to realize it was in my hand. These pumps are set up to provide a controlled amount of morphine every six minutes, so it's impossible to overdose, but I certainly tried. I don't know if I was drowsy from my self-medicating efforts or if one of the nurses put something else in my IV, but I barely remember the doctors giving me fuzzy directions—"sit up," "hold still," "lift your head," and so on. Gail told me later that the process took almost an hour. The device is cumbersome, with several separate parts that have to be bolted together. I don't remember a lot of the process, but I do remember when the four pointed screws were screwed into my skull. The step when the screws pierced the skin wasn't so bad, but the crunching sensation of the skin being crushed between the screw and the skull was definitely uncomfortable. I remember telling them not to over-tighten the screws; I guess I thought they needed my drug-addled advice. As it turned out, they knew what they were doing. They even used a torque wrench to make certain that exactly six inch-pounds of pressure were applied to each screw.

That was the only time I got to see Dr. Burke, and I really couldn't see him well then. All I remember is that he was a tall, slender man, and I'm not even sure what his voice sounded like. Either he and Dr. Maserati didn't talk much, or they were using their quiet voices so I couldn't hear what they were planning to do to me next as they installed the halo. The only other contact I had with Dr. Burke was to request a brief bit of biographical information, months later, through an email. When I asked if he had a particularly compelling reason for choosing medicine as a career, he responded, "Because the Pirates already had a shortstop." You've got to like someone with a sense of humor like that.

The rest of Tuesday was spent trying to overcome the panic that was smothering me. I couldn't move my head! I mean, I could not move my head at all! And when you can't move, the only thing you think about is how much you want to move. This irrational fear was something I had never experienced before. *Whatever made me think I could keep this horrible thing on for at least three months?* Thank goodness for the morphine pump; it provided several minutes or even half an hour of relief, but as soon as I regained consciousness I would panic again because of the immobility. These panic attacks only lasted for about the first twelve hours, and then the feelings of suffocation began to subside.

The next problem I noticed was that this torture apparatus made it really difficult to swallow. Although we aren't usually aware of it, the head moves forward and backward slightly when we swallow, so immobilizing the head makes this routine task a real challenge. Do you know how many pills you have to take when you're in the ICU? I don't either, but it's a lot, and the nurses keep bringing them all through the day and night. Every sip of water, every pill, and every bit of pureed food made me feel as though I was going to choke. This problem would eventually ease, but it was probably two or three weeks before I found a way to adjust my swallowing technique. I say I adjusted my technique, but maybe I just got used to swallowing the only way that I could.

My first two nights in the ICU (Saturday and Sunday) had been horrible, or so I thought. In addition to the constant checking and monitoring and the pain of the injuries, I had other factors to contend with—the neck brace, the emotional distress of the accident, the inability to move, the leg pressure cuffs, and the constant noise. All these made sleep hard to come by. But Monday night was worse, because of postsurgical pain and the drainage tube in my throat, and Tuesday represented a level of discomfort that I hadn't thought possible. Besides causing panic attacks and difficulty with swallowing, the halo also made it absolutely impossible to get comfortable. Even my arms hurt because they were resting against the hard plastic plates that covered my chest and back and formed part of the halo. I had never been so miserable, so uncomfortable, and so utterly helpless in my entire life. The night seemed to last forever as I lay there and watched the minutes go by on the wall clock, waiting for my wife and family to return the next day. I certainly had a lot of time to think, talk to myself, and talk to God.

There was one more medical development on Tuesday, but it involved Gail. Gail's injuries may have been less severe than mine, but they were nonetheless very painful. She had been discharged from the hospital late Sunday afternoon with cracks in two of her cervical vertebrae and a small tear in each rotator cuff. All this was painful, especially the shoulders, but she also kept complaining of pain in the rib area of her back. With the help of Jack Rocco, an orthopedic surgeon in Altoona who's a friend of our family, Gail was taken for some additional x-rays. Sure enough, there were two cracked ribs that weren't found initially, but fortunately none of her injuries required surgery. However, Gail did have to wear a "Miami J" cervical collar for almost three months, to give the cracks in her neck time to heal.

—

Tuesday night would be my last night in the ICU. Four nights in the intensive care unit wouldn't seem like a long time by some standards—I'm thinking of our wounded warriors—but for me they were the longest and most painful nights of my life. But on the positive side, the C6/C7 cervical fusion had been accomplished without any complications, and my neck was at least temporarily stabilized, now that the halo was on. Only time would tell whether the broken C1 vertebrae would heal, but I was determined not to dwell on that problem. Right now all I could deal with was one day at a time.

Eight

Highway to Hell

On Wednesday they moved me one floor below the ICU to what is called the SPCU, or Surgical Progressive Care Unit. The morphine pump I had relied on was taken away, but those awful leg cuffs were removed too, and nighttime monitoring now became less frequent and less intrusive. In the ICU they check on you every hour around the clock, but in the SPCU they would only be checking on me every two to three hours. Also, they now expected me to sit up in bed and start to use a walker. It's shocking how weak you become after lying in a hospital bed for just four days. The combination of weakness, pain, and imbalance (created by the halo) made walking a real challenge—I think thirty feet is all I managed on the first attempt.

Another thing that changed with the move to the SPCU was that I was encouraged to eat. I don't remember eating anything in the ICU; in fact, even my liquid intake was limited—I remember sucking water off a sponge on a stick. I had no appetite and could only take one or two small bites of the pureed food they brought. All told, I lost seventeen pounds between Saturday evening and the following Friday morning.

In conjunction with my new exercise regimen (walking thirty feet a couple of times), I was also encouraged to get out of bed—with assistance—and drag my IVs with me into the bathroom. This was a major step in the right direction, since now I would be able to brush my teeth again. After a few days of total helplessness, accomplishing even simple tasks was encouraging. One thing I'll warn you about, however, is not to get out of bed when the nurses say you can't—the alarm is really loud!

Other than setting off the bed alarm, not much happened on Wednesday. The staff and nurses were different, since I had been moved to a different floor, but the level of care was still good. Nurses work very hard, especially those on third shift, and most of the care that patients receive is from nurses rather than doctors. We've all heard horror stories of mistakes and poor care, but my experiences were positive. I think it helps when family members are present, both as a source of support for the patient and as a second set of eyes for the staff. For those unfortunate enough to end up in the ER and the ICU without family or friends nearby, the role played by the nurses is even more important. I talked to all my nurses as often as possible, and asked questions about them and their families. I did this especially during the long night hours for a somewhat selfish reason—I wanted them to stay in my room and talk with me. I wish I had written down all their names, along with a paragraph or two, to better remember the personal stories they shared.

Our nephew Luke—the second son of my wife's sister and her husband—came to visit on Wednesday. Luke had just graduated from college in Wisconsin, and he had the day off from his temporary summer job near Philadelphia. We hadn't seen him since Nathan and Alex's wedding four years before. He's an outgoing young man with an ebullient personality; he also has a smartphone, and he knows how to use it. "Here, Uncle Chuck," he said, "Say hi to Mom and Dad"—and the next moment I was talking to Vickie and Wynne via Skype. Pretty neat! The bad part was that they were able to see me, too. Don't ever let your nephew put you on a video conference call if you're wearing a halo in the hospital—you probably won't look good, either. Before my slowly reacting brain was able to explain why we might not want to do that again, the little screen was in front of my face once more—this time I was looking at Uncle Vaughan and Aunt Gail in Florida...

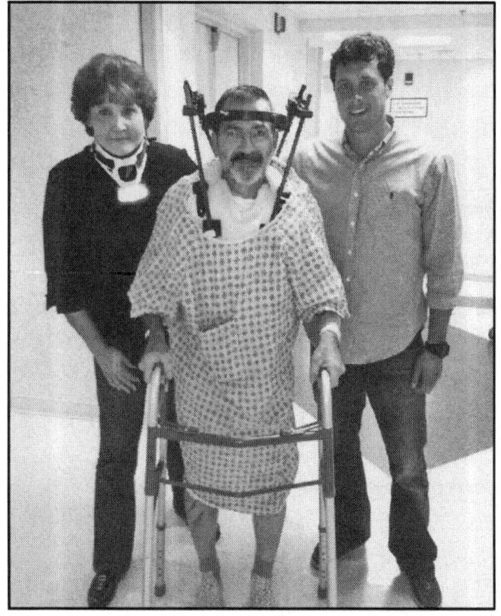

Gail, me, and Luke as I begin my thirty-foot walk.

Wednesday led to Wednesday night, with all of its associated discomforts and my obvious attempts to forestall the loneliness by keeping the nurses and staff in my room. Eventually Thursday morning arrived, and we learned that this would be my last full day in the hospital. On Friday they would be transporting me to a rehabilitation facility back home in Lynchburg. This news was both exciting and scary. I was anxious to return to more familiar surroundings, but I wasn't looking forward to the five-and-a-half-hour drive. I knew that Nathan and Alex had borrowed an Escalade from Alex's parents, but I wasn't sure that would work. I was barely able to get out of bed with assistance and walk a short distance. *How am I supposed to get into an SUV? How will I position myself once inside? What if there's an emergency?* Nate, Alex, and Gail wouldn't know what to do if something went wrong. All of them are smart and capable people, but they aren't medical professionals, and I didn't want to put this responsibility on them.

The ambulance transport that the hospital was recommending sounded like the best idea. I would be rolled out on a "bed" that would be secured in the back of the ambulance—taking care of the accessibility problem—and the two people transporting me would both be paramedics. And of course Nate, Alex, and Gail would be following in the Escalade. What could possibly go wrong?

We were scheduled to load up and leave around 6:30 a.m. on Friday, but a last-minute legal issue caused a delay. (The paramedics needed written permission to give me some medication while I was in transit.) That problem was finally resolved, and eventually they were ready to load me into the ambulance, but unfortunately the paperwork debacle was just a prelude to what I could expect the rest of the day.

As soon as Gail met the ambulance driver and her assistant, she learned that they were EMTs, not paramedics. Gail was not happy; she had been told by the ambulance transport company the day before that at least one of the staff would be a paramedic. Well, it was too late to do anything now. (At least the driver had been an EMT for over twenty years, and she sounded knowledgeable. Her helper, a young man, had been in the business for around five years.)

Next, I saw that I was going to be placed on the typical transporting gurney that's found in the back of every ambulance. Why had I assumed that something more like a hospital bed would be used? You remember that these gurneys are narrow, poorly padded, and ridiculously uncomfortable. They may be perfect for quick local transport in an emergency, but I never expected one to be used for such a long trip. I had been miserable in a hospital bed, and now one of those was going to seem luxurious. *You've got to be kidding me; five and half hours on one of these things?* The EMTs explained that this was the only type of bed that could be locked into the sides of the vehicle. This trip was looking worse by the minute. The thought crossed my mind to call the whole fiasco off and take my chances in the Escalade, but huge issues would arise with a change of plan: The fee for the ambulance had been paid with a credit card, the hospital had not approved our personal transport idea, and I still had reservations about putting full responsibility for my care on the shoulders of my family. It looked as though I'd be taking another ambulance ride.

As the hospital staff was getting me settled in the ambulance, Nathan spent several minutes talking with Kim, the driver, and explaining that her GPS would probably direct her to Route 501 when she was about an hour away from Lynchburg. This route would take her through the town of Buena Vista and over some of the most twisting mountain roads she had ever seen—not the best plan for a large ambulance bearing a patient with a broken neck. There was a better way with straighter roads that involved taking Route 29 and traveling through Charlottesville. Nate went over and over this plan with her, and she assured him that she understood. Just for the fun of it—which route do you think we ended up taking?

The hasty notes that follow were made by my daughter-in-law Alexandra, an attorney, during and immediately after the trip. I decided not to alter them, feeling that a transcription of her original notes provide a better sense of the frustration, stress, fear, and anger than anything else could. For me, the worst part of the ride wasn't the pain, but rather the thought that after all I had just survived I was probably now going to die in an ambulance crash.

> Friday, June 21, 2013
>
> Chuck was transported to Virginia Baptist Hospital via (REDACTED) Ambulance transport. Left at approximately 7:50 am; arrived at approximately 1:30 pm. EMTs were Kim (the driver) and Bo.
>
> The ambulance transport was terrible. We observed the vehicle swerving off the road, crossing the fog line and rumble strip, and at one point both tires were on the shoulder. The driver quickly swerved back on the road. Chuck felt all of this. He inquired about it and Bo told Chuck that they were avoiding something in the road. However, we were directly behind them in the Escalade and never saw any obstacles in the road. After two terrible swerves Nate sped up beside the ambulance and honked the horn. The lady just smiled at him. Nate contacted the manager (Rodney) at the transport company and informed him of her poor driving. He said he would call Kim. At one point the ambulance slowed down to 45

mph in a 70 mph zone to let Chuck urinate. Chuck requested that they pull off but they would not. Even though Nate told the ambulance driver not to take 501 through Buena Vista multiple times and she acted like she was going to listen, she did not. When we came to the point to exit for Interstate 64, Nate honked the horn and flashed the lights at the driver, but she did not exit. Instead, she took the exit that went through Buena Vista to 501 and it was terrible. The roads are extremely curvy. Chuck was nauseated because of the stupidity of the driver. Consequently, he was unable to take his pain medicine. Once Chuck was safely in the Virginia Baptist Hospital Acute Rehab, Nate had some words with the ambulance driver and EMT. (Nate) I directed my comments mainly towards Kim (driver) and started by asking her, "Do you understand why I requested that you not take the Buena Vista route?" (Kim) "I had no idea the roads were that bad." (Nate) "Kim, I told you 5 times that we needed to take the Interstate 64 route to Charlottesville, then come down 29 to Lynchburg." (Kim) "Well if I had known they were that curvy I would have never taken that route." I reiterated to her that I was from the area and knew exactly how curvy the roads were and this is why I directed her on the appropriate roads to take. (Kim) "I was only aware of I-64 going into Norfolk." (Nate) "I was behind you the entire time and I assume you check your mirrors as most drivers do. When we approached the exit to get on I-64 East, I was in the exit lane, flashing my lights and beeping the horn. You paid no attention and continued on the path as directed by the GPS even though I had told you numerous times that this was not the best way." I stressed to her how displeased I was with her blatant disregard for the patient's comfort, especially since the injury was a broken neck. I then brought up the terrible driving that occurred. (Nate) "Kim, can you explain to me the multiple times that you ran off the road?" (Kim) "I had to stretch my shoulders [gesturing a turn to the right]." (Nate) "Well, that may have been the cause for one of the occurrences, but you had the entire van out of the lane twice, hit the rumble-strip 4–5 times and rode the fog line for most of the trip." (Kim) "It was a long trip and you just sort of get locked in to the road." (Nate) "Kim, that is ridiculous! You are supposed to be a professional driver. All you do is drive and you can't keep the vehicle on the road. I am not a 'professional' driver, and not once did my vehicle's tires touch the rumble-strips. On one particular instance, where you swerved off the road and jerked the van back to the left, I honked my horn, not knowing if you fell asleep, and then I accelerated up beside you in the left lane. You looked over and I threw my hands up. You then proceeded to turn your head to the left, look at me and smile. Your driving skills are terrible and there is no excuse. I have already called your manager (Rodney), and I will be making another call momentarily."

This harrowing ambulance ride, complete with pictures, was documented for several reasons: First, the company needed to know about the unsafe driving practices of its employee; second, if there had been an accident, someone would have had to explain, and prove, what had happened; and last, it was a very expensive ride that our insurance would not cover. We eventually came to a financial agreement with the ambulance company that was acceptable to everyone—and was a more accurate reflection of the service we received.

But the final outcome of this wild ride was that I was back in Lynchburg, and delivered to the Virginia Baptist Hospital Acute Rehabilitation Center. I was exhausted from the trip and simply wanted to sleep, but it was still early in the day, and this rehab center was not known for letting patients rest. After registering me, they took me to my room, gave me a quick physical, showed me how to use a wheelchair, and gave me a copy of my schedule. Then we headed off to an exercise room for my evaluation. They wanted to establish a baseline right away so they would know where to begin on Monday. *These guys don't waste any time.* CJ and Megan came to meet us when we first arrived, but the staff kept me so busy from the moment I was rolled through the door that I barely remember talking to them.

Finally, around 5:00 or 6:00 p.m., I was taken back to my room. I still had no appetite, and all I wanted to do was rest. That night my room was much quieter than the ICU and SPCU rooms I had just left in Altoona, and they actually closed the door to block out light and noise from the hallway. That, combined with exhaustion and pain pills, helped me to sleep better than I had since the accident. *This must be heaven.*

Saturday morning Dr. Jim Stutesman woke me when he was making his rounds. Jim is a tall, distinguished man with a friendly voice, and he made it a point to encourage every patient. He asked me how I was feeling and mentioned that he, too, is a pilot—in fact, the next morning he brought me a couple of his aviation magazines. When we got around to talking about the nerve pain I'd been experiencing in my right hand, he suggested Neurontin, and I started the minimum dose later that day.

That morning I put on real clothes for the first time in a week. Alex had gone to Wal-Mart on Friday and found some extra-large shirts for me to wear over the halo. So, sporting khaki-style shorts, sneakers, and my very bulky shirt, I was ready for the day.

Breakfast began at 8:00 a.m., and I actually felt hungry—maybe because I had slept better on Friday night. Patients had the choice of eating in their rooms or going to the community room and eating with everyone else. Most preferred the social contact, so the community room was usually full at mealtimes. I was still adjusting to the halo, and most of my upper body hurt—I moved very slowly and needed help getting into the wheelchair—but at least I was able to roll myself down the hall to join the other patients for breakfast.

I still vividly remember what I had for breakfast: scrambled eggs, bacon, coffee, juice, and buttered toast. It was the first real food I had had in a week, and it smelled enticingly good. It tasted good, too, and I ate at least half of it. We all stayed in our wheelchairs during meals, so when I finished, all I had to do was roll myself back to my room. I'd only been back for about ten minutes when I started pushing the call button, and telling the nurse I needed some anti-nausea medicine… fast. She came immediately and I swallowed it quickly—but it didn't help. Luckily, I was sitting in the wheelchair right beside a sink. *That wasn't any fun at all.* If I thought swallowing with the halo on was hard, bringing it back up was even harder. I wondered what would happen if I really choked, because it's not like someone could grab me and do the Heimlich maneuver when my torso was encased in this hard plastic shell. *Wouldn't that be a bummer—survive a plane wreck, and the highway to hell, only to choke to death a week later!*

Regular therapy sessions were not scheduled over the weekend, which was good, because after Friday's ride, the only thing I wanted to do was rest. It was nice to be back in our home town, where CJ and Megan could visit every day along with Gail, Nathan, and Alex. They came by as often as they could, and that was the bright spot of my day. The downside was that I wouldn't be seeing Mom, Dad, and my brother Dan, the way I had in Altoona.

I'm not certain what time my family arrived Saturday morning, but by the time lunch was ready at the Center, they had left to find their own lunch. I don't remember what I had to eat, but I do remember the outcome. *Why does everything make me sick?* Maybe my stomach was just reacting to not eating for a week, or maybe all the pills I took in the morning were making it upset—I didn't know. Later that day I took an anti-nausea pill before dinner and was finally able to keep that small meal down.

It was on Sunday that the realization of how long-term my predicament was finally started to settle in. The six days in the Altoona hospital had been a blur of emotions, operations, nurses, beeping monitors, and drugs. Friday had been a day of change, moving from Altoona to the rehab facility in Lynchburg. Saturday was spent getting adjusted to my new surroundings. But on Sunday it hit me—*I'm not going to be getting better soon, and I'll never be exactly the way I was before the accident*. The depression that would attack relentlessly later, when I was home by myself, was beginning its insidious assault.

But on Monday I was at least feeling (and looking) better than I had on my return trip to Lynchburg. Three nights of intermittent sleep, plus three small meals kept down on Sunday, had raised my spirits. I was also anticipating the beginning of my therapy sessions, which lasted all Monday morning and continued, after a break for lunch, until 4:00 p.m. My routine consisted of hand strength and dexterity exercises, standing, walking, and navigating stairs. The rehab therapists and their assistants knew that patients would not get better without effort, and they were very good at making people put forth that effort. My physical therapist was a man named Lamont. He, the occupational therapist (Pat), and her rehab assistant (Betty) were all proficient and patient as they worked to bring a level of normality back to the lives of people affected by accidents, operations, or strokes.

Most of the patients, I noticed, were at the rehab facility because of a stroke, and most were between the ages of fifty and eighty. One friendly guy I met, Steve, had recently had back surgery and was wearing a large plastic brace that covered his entire torso. My best guess is that Steve was around fifty. He was very polite and instantly likeable; he had a booming voice and was trying hard to maintain a positive outlook. The neurosurgeon who had performed his surgery was the same doctor I would be meeting in about six weeks, and Steve was able to provide valuable advance information about him.

By Tuesday I felt as though I had accomplished the goals the rehab center had established for me. I was able to get in and out of bed by myself, take care of bathroom needs, walk with a walker, navigate stairs, and get in and out of a car. This progress, along with the fact that I had been moved from my private room and now had a roommate, caused me to tell Dr. Jim that I was ready to go home on Wednesday. The staff had originally thought I would need to stay until Friday, but I assured them that I'd be fine at home and would definitely rest better in my own bed. After discussing this request with my physical therapist, they all agreed that one more session of therapy on Wednesday morning—focused on using stairs and getting in and out of a car—should be sufficient.

On Wednesday morning Gail, Nate, and Alex all came to the rehab center so that the doctor and the therapist could give them some special instructions. After a couple of hours the session was complete, the paperwork was signed, and my few belongings were loaded up. After thanking the doctor, the therapist, and the staff, I said goodbye to a few of the patients I'd gotten to know. Their struggles as victims of stroke would keep them at the rehab facility for about two to four weeks, on average, and fortunately there was a good chance most of them would regain much of their mobility. I pray that they have.

Riding in a car felt strange as we left the rehab facility and headed toward home. It had only been eleven days since the accident, but it seemed a lot longer; much had happened already, and even more was still unknown. Dr. Maserati in Pennsylvania was my trusted and capable neurosurgeon, but now I'd be meeting a new doctor in Virginia who would be taking responsibility for the next step in my care. Little did I know that I would also be meeting a third neurosurgeon whose name I'd not even heard yet. He would be performing a rare surgery that at the time we thought had only been done twice before in China, and it was going to have a profound impact on my life.

Nine

Rare Operation

HAVE YOU EVER NOTICED HOW HOME JUST FEELS DIFFERENT AFter you've been away for a few weeks? You see your possessions from a visitor's perspective—one that isn't blurred by mundane familiarity. That's how I felt when I walked—carefully—through our front door on June 26. That feeling of disconnection, coupled with questions of uncertainty about the future, made everything seem odd. I had built the house back in 1996 and did most of the maintenance on it myself, so there were always little projects going on. At the time of the accident we were planning to install new countertops in the kitchen, along with a new sink and appliances, and the tools I intended to use for that job were lined up on the shop shelves. Not being able to use these familiar implements, at least for now, made them seem foreign. I've always had diverse interests and built things that allowed me to accumulate some nice tools. Now they were useless to me, and I would have to rely on someone else to even cut the grass.

Fortunately, Nathan and Alex were able to stay with us a few more days to help out; they had been by our side since June 16, and they could stay until the 29th. CJ lives in Lynchburg and had been taking care of all the paperwork associated with the accident; now he would also end up helping with yard work and other tasks. Gail's sister Vickie and her son Caleb also offered to come down from Wisconsin to help: They arrived on July 2 and stayed almost three weeks. What an encouragement and boost to our morale they all were! Everything was appreciated—not only practical help, like meals, transportation, and yard work, but little encouragements, like recommending a book or just talking for awhile.

I'd been on the phone with my family back in Pennsylvania almost every day since we returned to Virginia, and when my dad heard that Vickie and Caleb were leaving on the 22nd, he also offered to help. He arrived right after Vickie left and was great company for several days. Gail had returned to work with the Roanoke County School System by then, and being at home by yourself when you're unable to drive is enough to bore you to tears. I have a much greater sense of empathy now for older folks who lose their independence. I used to think that a week or two at home without the usual home responsibilities would be enjoyable, and it might be, under normal circumstances. But when you're stumbling around with a halo on your head, and pain pills clouding your mind, you're not able to do the reading, writing, and desk work that you were hoping to do. So Dad was good company and an able chauffeur as he drove me around taking care of errands. He even fixed the mailbox that I'd been intending to repair for the last year.

This picture was taken at home three months after the accident and right before the second surgery.

A week after Dad left, on August 5, Gail took me to meet Dr. Dilan Ellegala in his office. This would be my first contact with a doctor since I had left the rehab center almost six weeks before. The first thing Dr. Ellegala wanted to know was whether anyone had checked the tightness of the four screws on the halo since it had been secured to my head. When I replied in the negative, he smiled and said that would need to be done. Then he brought out a tool I was familiar with but never expected to see in a medical context—a torque wrench. It was cleaner than the wrench in the typical mechanic's tool box, but it was still like every other torque wrench I'd ever seen. He said that the screws needed to be kept tightened at a level of 6 inch-pounds per screw. *I don't think I'm going to like this.*

If you've never used a torque wrench before, the principle is simple: You set the tool to the desired tightness and then place the tool on the bolt or screw. Then, as you tighten the screw and it reaches the designated tightness setting, it makes a loud metallic "click" and stops tightening. Sounds pretty simple, doesn't it, until you remember that the screw being tightened is going into my skull. Every sensation or vibration that went through that screw was multiplied and transmitted to my head—and when the wrench went "click," a jolt shot from my skull all the way down to my feet.

Once the four halo screws were checked for proper torque, Dr. Ellegala started to discuss my condition and offer his opinion on my injuries. He had spent several minutes looking over the CT scans and the MRI. He tried to be positive and assuage my concern that the widest C1 break would never heal, but it still came down to what Dr. Maserati had told me in Pennsylvania—"Only time would tell."

Dr. Ellegala's opinions and educated guesses were obviously important to me. He is the Medical Director of Neuroscience Services at Centra Health (Centra is the largest medical group in the Lynchburg area) and a highly qualified physician. He later introduced me to the newest neurosurgeon specializing in spine surgery and neurotrauma at the Centra Health Neuroscience Institute—Dr. Hugh Gill.

When I first met Dr. Gill I liked him immediately. Hugh Gill was born in New Orleans in 1972, the youngest child—and only boy—in a family of five children. After graduating from high school in 1990, he decided to put off going to college and instead joined the Marine Corps. It was after this period of full-time military service that he entered the University of California at San Diego, followed by medical school at Tulane. By the time he finished his various residencies and internships at Georgetown, he was married with three sons and well established in his chosen field of medicine.

Dr. Gill had just moved to Lynchburg a month or two before from Washington, D.C., where he had completed his residency at Medstar Washington Hospital Center and an internship at Medstar Georgetown University Hospital. The Medstar complex of medical facilities is known for its neuroscience and neurosurgery centers. His new title at Centra Health was Director of Centra Neuroscience Institute's Minimally Invasive Spine Services. In just six short weeks I'd learn how valuable his finely honed skills and years of preparation would be to me.

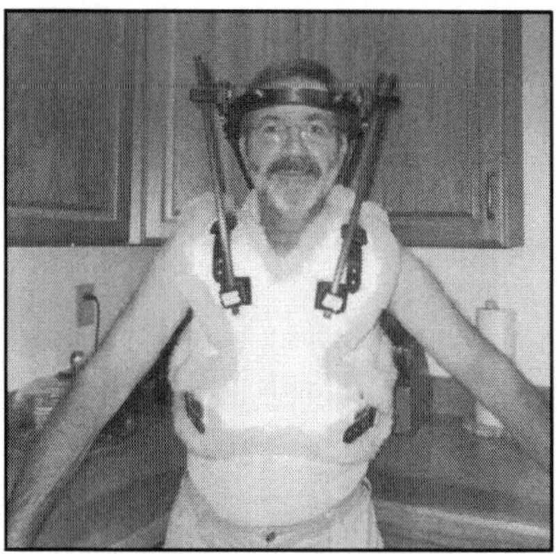

Back home in the kitchen about
a month after the accident.

When we left Dr. Gill's office, Gail and I returned to our now-empty house. After seven weeks we had healed sufficiently to be able to take care of ourselves, and our family caretakers had returned to their own homes. I had adapted to my halo enough to be left by myself while Gail was at work. You know, I don't even like saying those words, *left by myself.* I wasn't able to drive, and I was still taking pain meds, so I was tired most of the day. I was unable to do anything physical and incapable of focusing sufficiently to be able to write or do anything mentally demanding. My time alone was not going to be the most life-threatening or the most painful part of this whole experience, but it was going to be the most mentally challenging. And by mentally challenging, I mean "depressing."

I could partially relate to this type of loneliness through two prior experiences. The first was when I was a young graduate student, living by myself and attending the University of Pittsburgh. I didn't know anyone in the city, and for the first couple of months I understood what it was like to be "lonely in a crowd." The second experience was observing my mother-in-law. After my father-in-law passed away, Dorothy lived by herself for several years before finally giving in, selling her home, and living alternately with her two daughters, Gail in Virginia and Vickie in Wisconsin (I'll let you deduce which state she chose during the winter). Eventually her health worsened and she wasn't able to travel back and forth, and when that happened, she came to live with Gail and me full time. She was never a complainer, but she did bemoan the loss of her independence and ability to drive. I wish now that I had been more sympathetic, but until I wasn't able to drive at all for five months, I just didn't know how hard that can be.

Compound my physical restrictions with the uncertainty of the future, and it was challenging to maintain a positive attitude. Thankfully, between family, friends, business associates, church acquaintances, and neighbors, we did have our share of encouragement. Everyone who helped was appreciated, and though I could never thank everyone here, because I'm sure I would leave too many out, those who supported us were the main reason I was able to get out of bed each morning. A loose paraphrase of a verse in Corinthians says that we have been comforted so that we will be better able to comfort and encourage others. I've known that passage for a long time, but I seldom took the time to be a good encourager. That's now changed because understanding leads to empathy, and empathy leads to compassion. I recognize and have a better grasp now of several things I never understood before.

—

Slowly four weeks passed since first meeting Dr. Gill, and on September 4th I went to Central Virginia Imaging to have a CT scan—followed by a consultation with the good doctor. It had been almost three months since the installation of the halo, and now we were going to find out if any healing had taken place.

For almost three months I had not picked up anything heavier than a gallon of milk. I had been careful with every step I took, walking slowly and purposefully around the house in order to not stumble over the cat or a loose rug. I had always held onto something with both hands when getting in and out of the bathtub. I traveled in a car only when necessary because I knew that even a small accident could damage something that was starting to heal. And I continued to pray. I wanted desperately for my neck to heal and for everything to be like it used to be, but more than that I had to keep everything in perspective and try to maintain a good attitude.

My neck could never be stable if the C1 vertebrae remained cracked, and the only solution—if it hadn't healed on its own—would be to permanently fuse my skull with the C1 and C2 vertebrae. Definitely a life-changer—no more motorcycles, no more flying, no more hunting or rifle shooting. I wasn't even certain about my ability to drive or to continue working in the home-inspection/construction business.

My mind was racing as Gail and I waited for Dr. Gill to come into the examination room. The CT scan had been taken a few hours earlier, and now the results were being reviewed in the office down the hall. I was too nervous to sit and instead started pacing. The room smelled like alcohol, and between the examining table, two chairs, the storage cabinet with sink, and the corner desk with a computer on it, there wasn't a lot of space. Outside it was a sunny September day, but I wasn't enjoying it as I paced back and forth.

After around ten minutes Rob, the physician's assistant, and Jennifer, the nurse practitioner, knocked and came into the room.

They greeted us and then pulled up the CT scan on the computer. They talked in low voices as Jennifer manipulated the picture until she had just the right angle to show my broken vertebrae. Then, without fanfare or excitement, Rob said he had both good news and bad news—"the small break has healed and the big one has not." That was it. "The doctor will be here in a minute," Rob said, and they both shook our hands and left. I felt numb, and there wasn't enough air in the room. I kept looking at the picture on the screen and even my untrained eye could see the jagged break. *This is bad, this is very bad*. I told Gail that things were going to change now, as I resumed pacing. Not being able to do the things I'd enjoyed all my life would be bad enough, but what was I going to do with my business?

When Dr. Gill came in, he sat on the short rolling chair in front of the computer. We both looked at the screen, and he pointed to what I had already seen. I said it appeared as though I'd be getting my neck fused, just as I'd feared. I braced myself for his response, but he had some news I didn't expect. He said that normally the answer would be "yes," but that he'd been looking online and found a procedure that had been done just twice before in China, in which the broken C1 vertebrae halves had been pulled together with a screw. Since the smaller break in C1 appeared to be healed, he might be able to try this rare procedure on the larger break. I took a deep breath and thanked God for a faint spark of hope. Obviously this could not have been attempted if there were still two breaks in the same vertebrae. Maybe three months of wearing this appalling halo would prove to be a blessing after all.

After everything had a minute to sink in, I asked why this procedure was so rare. He explained that over 95% of those who break the C1 vertebrae in this way are either dead or quadriplegic; there simply aren't many patients left to practice on. He went on to explain the risks involved with such a surgery, including several ways the operation could fail: The screw could strip when tightened; the bone might not be sufficiently solid at the point of contact with the screw; or there could be too much tissue or debris between the broken halves to be able to draw them together. It was also possible that the edges of the break could have already healed to such a degree that they would not knit even if put in direct contact with one another. Last, even if the surgery seemed successful initially, it was possible that the screw might pull loose in a week or two.

He, of course, had never done this procedure before, and he wasn't painting a very rosy picture. But at least there was a chance! I wouldn't have to be fused just yet, and I was willing to grasp at any straw, no matter how slender.

There would only be one opportunity to make this gamble work, and we needed to attempt it right away. Dr. Gill explained that he would have all the parts necessary to do a total neck fusion in the operating room on the day he attempted the new procedure. A three-inch vertical incision had to be made in the back of my neck, and in the event the screw did not hold, there was no sense in wasting a perfectly good three-inch incision. I signed some papers and gave my approval. Plans were made for the operation to take place in one week, on September 11. In seven days I would either wake up with hope still intact or with a solidly fused neck.

—

I've already talked so much about stress, uncertainty, depression, hope, and conflicting emotions throughout this whole ordeal that I hate to describe what the next week was like, especially in light of what happened on the day of the operation. I was required to be at the hospital two hours before the surgery, so that meant I needed to be there at 5:00 a.m. It takes forty minutes to get to the hospital from our home in the country, so Gail and I were both up by 3:30 a.m.

We arrived on time and went directly to the admissions office to complete the paperwork. Then we were taken to a pre-op room, where I used an anti-bacterial cloth to sterilize my upper body and then changed into the infamous open-backed surgical gown. The whole process just did not seem real at that early hour—and in such an austere and unfamiliar place. The staff worked hard to put me at ease, though, and the warm blankets definitely helped. CJ and Nathan came around 6:00, and we got to talk awhile before it was time for the orderly to roll me down to the operating prep room. Ten or twelve friends had come to support Gail, and they were watching for her as she left me and went into the waiting room. We have some good friends who will use any excuse for a party, and Lois Williams even made a coffee cake. I think they were having way too much fun without me.

Once in the prep room, the nurses busied themselves getting me ready, and then the anesthesiologist stopped by to talk. I had been anticipating this pre-op conversation, because I had such unpleasant memories of that intubation in Pennsylvania. I told the anesthesiologist how the first operation three months ago had been horrible because I had to remain conscious while being intubated. I also explained that a friend from church, who is an anesthesiologist, had told me that an instrument called a glide scope could make the process much easier this time around. This seemed to be agreeable, and he affirmed that I would not have to be awake when he started his work. Thank the Lord, because that part of the operation was the one thing I had truly been dreading.

After he left, the nurse put something into my IV to relax me, and I kept waiting to be rolled next door to the operating room. I don't know how long I waited, but it must have been awhile because I started thinking that the relaxing medicine was going to wear off and I would be fully alert when rolled into the OR. Eventually someone came in and told me there was a problem. Apparently Dr. Gill had expected the hospital to have a piece of equipment that could secure my halo to the operating table, but they couldn't locate one. They had even been calling hospitals in Roanoke and Charlottesville, but no luck. It soon became apparent that this operation just wasn't going to happen today.

When Dr. Gill came to talk with me, he was very apologetic. He had only been operating in the Lynchburg General Hospital for a short while, and at his previous hospital, this piece of equipment was readily available. What could he say? It was a mistake. The good news, however, was that the sedative had worn off, I was now wide awake, and there was still some of Lois's coffee cake left…it was delicious.

We rescheduled for one week later at the same early hour. (I didn't mention it before, but Dr. Ellegala was also going to be in the operating room with Dr. Gill—I think he wanted to see this unusual procedure.) So on the following Wednesday all of us—me, my family, the doctors, the nurses, the orderlies, even our friends—came back for another try. Two things changed, though: Lois made something different to eat, and I had a new anesthesiologist. The second part of that scenario almost became a problem. When I was in the pre-op room getting the IVs inserted, the different anesthesiologist came in and began explaining how I would have to remain conscious while being intubated. *No, no, no, that's not what I was told last week.* I explained how my broken neck had been stabilized by the halo, my anesthesiologist friend had told me about the glide scope, and last week's anesthesiologist had assured me I would not have to be awake. I tried to be respectful, but I was determined not to go through that choking experience again. He had me open my mouth so he could see how the airway was tilted and then said that yes, he did believe he would be able to put me under before doing the intubation. Good thing I spoke up, because *that* would have been an unpleasant surprise.

The operation took about two hours, and everything went well. In fact, it went exceedingly well, and Dr. Gill successfully performed a surgery that had been done by only a handful of other neurosurgeons in the world. He placed the screw in the proper position and applied just enough torque to draw the two broken halves of the C1 vertebrae together without over-tightening the screw and causing it to strip out. I had a three-inch incision in the back of my head with fourteen staples holding it together, but that was nothing. I actually now had a chance of regaining some mobility in my neck.

Dr. Gill came to my room later that afternoon and explained how the operation went. He said that although the two halves had not gone together perfectly, they were making contact at a few points. However, two big things could still go wrong: the screw could pull loose, or the healed edges of the break might not grow together even though they were touching. *OK, so we weren't quite out of the woods yet, but at least the trees weren't quite as dense.* He also said he would be back the next morning to take off the halo.

It was removed without sedation, and the pressure in my head was so intense when that first screw was loosened, I immediately asked Dr. Gill if he was turning the tool in the right direction. I think it came out, "Are you tightening that screw or what?" The remaining three screws weren't as bad, and the pressure subsided after several minutes. I didn't break into Dr. King's speech ("Free at last, free at last, thank God Almighty, I'm free at last"), but I wanted to. The freedom was short-lived, however, because a Miami J hard neck brace was put on right away. This was better than the halo, but it still wasn't a pleasure to wear. Gail had worn one for three months, and I had downplayed the severity of her discomfort when she complained about it. *After all, I'm the one with four screws in my head; I'm the one who's really uncomfortable here.* I should've kept my mouth shut. This thing is not comfortable at all, especially when you have to keep it on 24/7—*I'm sorry, Gail.*

Now would come one of the longest, most stressful months of this whole ordeal. For the next four weeks I would have to be especially careful not to do anything that might cause the screw to pull loose—and I had to remind myself every day that God loved me whether the bones ever grew back together or not. The date I was waiting for was October 15, when a CT scan and a follow-up visit with Dr. Gill would tell the tale. I'll spare you the daily stress I dealt with and just say, with gratitude, that the news on this upcoming visit would be much better than on that earlier appointment, when I first learned that the larger break in C1 had not healed. I continued to have a scan taken each month for the next two months, and both of those scans showed continued bone growth. So after six months—three with the halo on, and three with the Miami J hard collar on—the Miami J was removed, and I was able to look at myself in the mirror without some kind of brace on my neck.

I was anxious to begin rehabilitation to restore movement and recover the muscle lost in my neck, shoulders, arms, and back. However, Dr. Gill wanted to be cautious and wouldn't allow me to begin rehab for another three months. He suggested several easy stretching exercises, but that was about it. "This is unfamiliar ground we're covering," he said, "and the bone is secure but not completely healed."

The halo is off and the Miami J is on. CJ and Nate both grew beards and tried to look like me.

I probably wouldn't have been able to do much at rehab anyway—I just could not move my neck at first. By doing those small stretching exercises, things finally started to loosen up a little, but progress was slow. After three months of having the hard collar off, I had one more good CT scan showing additional bone growth, and Dr. Gill felt that rehab could be safely started. He wrote some sort of release form that I could now take to a rehabilitation facility. I should have realized earlier that no physical therapist would have touched me before I had this release. And no, I didn't think about going to see a physical therapist before I had Dr. Gill's approval—okay, yes I did...but only briefly!

Rehab Associates of Central Virginia has an office in Bedford, and both of the physical therapists, Richard Toms and Harrison Hunt, are excellent. Richard had recently completed his physical therapy degree from Lynchburg College, and his professional enthusiasm was encouraging. He and his wife had their first child within the first couple weeks of my beginning rehab, so for the next several weeks I enjoyed hearing about the follies and sleep loss of first-time parents. Richard is a few years younger than both of my sons, and since Gail and I don't have any grandchildren yet, I practiced giving my words of wisdom to him. I hope he enjoyed our brief talks as much as I did.

As I write this, it's been more than nine months from the day of the accident, and I continue to have a long way to go. My neck and shoulders are painful; mobility is limited and movement is stiff; my right hand remains numb and burning; and I'm only working a couple of days per week. But I'm still a grateful guy with a lot to be thankful for. I've learned some important lessons, and in several ways my life is far better than it was before.

I'll tell you why I say that and also share some of the lessons learned (I call them "borrowed insights") in the next four chapters.

PART

III

Behind all seen things lies something vaster; everything is but a path, a portal or a window opening on something other than itself.

— Antoine de Saint-Exupéry, *Wind, Sand and Stars*

The accident, the surgery, and the waiting gave me time to think a lot about health, attitudes, and relationships. It's so easy to base our attitudes on the condition of our bodies, but then aren't we setting ourselves up for failure and unhappiness? Eventually age, injury, or disease changes us all—it's just a matter of when. Then what will we do—never be happy again? Should we disparage and disavow God?

The Apostle Paul said, "But indeed, O man, who are you to reply against God? Will the thing formed say to him who formed it, 'Why have you made me like this?'" That's a difficult statement to comprehend, but who can claim to know everything about Nature, or about God, or if like Thomas Jefferson you can't quite decide, Nature's God? The world is full of difficult statements.

Across the expanse of our galaxy alone even the world's most brilliant intellect would be nothing more than an imperceptible speck of dust. On one hand, I admire the chutzpah of the creature who challenges the vastness of a cosmos that he believes created itself, but on the other hand my admiration turns to pity. As Chesterton said, "The trouble when people stop believing in God is not that they thereafter believe in nothing; it is that they thereafter believe in anything."

We shake our fist at God when we can't comprehend the inequities that surround us. We loudly claim there is no God if we witness the harming of the innocents. We rail at the wind when nature kills and maims indiscriminately. And all our lives we struggle to understand things that cannot be understood. Personally, I find life to be more comprehensible and tolerable when I believe there is a God and that He has a name. You might choose not to acknowledge any form of deity, but I can't do that.

We who believe in God espouse a point of view that provides answers to certain universal questions, such as where did I come from, why am I here, and where am I going? But now we also have an additional set of equally difficult questions by which we attempt to ascertain the mind and actions of God. Some of these can be just about impossible to get your head around. And if you come up with a universally acceptable answer for that whole "sovereignty of God and free will of man" thing, please give me a call.

Promoting what I believe has not been the reason for my writing; however, long-held religious beliefs naturally come out when describing experiences that are so personal. My purpose has been to simply share an esoteric story about building and flying an airplane, surviving an accident that statistically should have killed or paralyzed me, being the subject of a successful rare surgical procedure, and learning some lessons along the way.

So these last four chapters talk about things I've learned through the events of this past year. Most of them are simple observations, some are funny, and some are serious. I'm not a philosopher, counselor, or theologian, but I've had a few unusual experiences that forced me to slow down and think about my attitudes toward flying, family, God, and life in general. I hope they help you to do the same.

Ten

Borrowed Insights on Flying

Fly the Plane and Stay Alert Through the End of the Landing

YOU KNOW, I REALLY TRIED TO CONVINCE MYSELF, INITIALLY, THAT the gusting wind is what caused me to bounce when I landed the plane. And even though that was a factor, I don't think now that it was the only reason for what happened. The bad landing and the accident were all part of what had been, for me, my busiest day of flying ever. Earlier that morning my son, Nathan, and I had flown for about an hour and ten minutes. It was a great local flight in calm winds with a smooth landing at the end. Then an hour or two later, Gail and I took off for Pennsylvania. This was only a 250-nautical-mile trip, but it would be the first time I had ever ventured so far from my local area.

The flight, for me, was challenging. We had the Appalachian Mountains to cross in several places, and there was a low cloud base that kept us from getting as high above that rugged terrain as I would have liked. A week earlier we had turned back when attempting the same trip because the clouds were too low. Now we were bouncing along between the mountaintops and the clouds.

But after the mountains the flight smoothed out and I allowed my mind to wander. I was thinking about what the winds and clouds would be like on the return trip; I wanted to do a good landing with my family watching; I speculated on where we would go for lunch; and I wondered whether they had brought two cars to the airport, and if they hadn't, would we all fit in one? Then, as I watched the large runway—so much larger and flatter than my home airport's—slowly rise to meet us, I thought, *this landing should be easy*. I became relaxed and overconfident...never do that! Stay alert, and concentrate on flying the plane all the way through the end of the landing. Don't allow yourself to become distracted.

Avoid Straight-On Final Approaches Whenever Possible

Of all the factors that contributed to the accident, this may have been my worst mistake. I should have done what I had been doing 95% of the time in previous flights—determine pattern altitude, get into the pattern, do a standard down-wind, base and final approach, and then land. This would have prepared me mentally for the landing and helped me to stay focused. Everything was new on my first long trip, and inconsistency was not a good thing.

Five months after the accident I posted a thread on Vansairforce.net entitled, "You know it's a bad landing when you're upside down." This site is considered a daily must-read for anyone building or flying Van's RV planes. Doug Reeves does a stellar job with the site, and he has over 19,000 regular visitors. When I posted the thread about my accident, 13,500 people read it, and over 80 left comments. All the comments were kind, and none chastised me for the mistakes I'd made. (I guess they figured, "Why beat up a guy who just broke his neck?") In fact, most of the responses contained wishes for a speedy recovery, and many provided helpful suggestions and sound advice.

One valuable comment came from Bill Repucci of South Carolina, and I quote most of it here:

> One thing that I just do out of courtesy to other pilots is I never fly a straight-in approach to an uncontrolled field. There are a few reasons for this. First, there could be a no-radio plane in the pattern (Cub, T-Craft, etc.) that you will cut off. Second, an airplane with a radio, sitting on the ground, may/will not transmit that far and you could cut them off. Third, the FAA does not consider you in the pattern when more than three miles from the airport. And fourth, by flying the pattern the same every time, I have a set routine I follow for every landing. This consistency in approach helps make my landings "repeatable"/"consistent." They may not always be good landings, but at least they are consistent and repeatable.

Bill and I shared some emails after he read my post, and I appreciated his words of encouragement. Several shared similar stories of straight-in approaches that resulted in either accidents or some other issue. The bottom line is that inattention, complacency, or "trying something different" can all lead to an undesirable result. It's best to avoid those long finals and set up for landing by following the practice you're most familiar with.

When You're Upside Down Your First Thought is "Fire"

There were so many thoughts going through my head when I bounced the plane that it's hard to pick out the predominant one, but I think the fear of fire was right there at the top. As soon as the front landing gear gave way, we heard an awful scraping sound as the plane careened toward the side of the runway, and I envisioned sparks flying off the bent metal.

Another pilot who was popular among the RV crowd had an accident a few years ago and was badly burned. This tragedy, along with several other similar ones, was familiar to me and to most of the pilots I knew. Also, when installing the fuel lines and the pumps in the homebuilding process, you're given frequent reminders about how dangerous this liquid is and how precise your workmanship needs to be.

So while struggling to keep the plane on the runway, I reached over and pulled out the mixture control knob. The engine cut off, and a split second later we went into the grass, the bent gear dug into the soft dirt, the plane went up on its nose, and we flipped.

Hanging upside down by my shoulder harness and lap belt, I really wished I hadn't watched any of those WWII flying movies. *Was that gas?* Gail has a better sense of smell than I do, but I didn't want to put that thought in her head. Even if she smelled it, it wouldn't have made any difference. My heart was already pumping wildly and I knew *we needed to get out fast.*

One of the first things the firemen did when they arrived was to spray fire-retardant foam on the plane. They smelled the gas too, and didn't want to work at putting the plane upright before dealing with the threat of fire.

It's Difficult to Escape Even if the Canopy Shatters

Immediately upon impact, I realized that my right hand hurt and I wasn't able to grip anything. I could move it slightly, but beyond that, it was useless. I remember thinking—or maybe wishing—that I had simply broken my wrist, but the crushing pain in my neck when my head hit the ground probably meant otherwise. I still reached out to grab things for the first few minutes, but eventually it registered that I would only be working with one hand.

On the websites and forums that talk about my plane, a popular topic is how to get out if the plane flips. Remember, the bubble canopy either slides or tips up, and if the plane is resting upside down on this canopy, you obviously aren't able to open it. Some pilots advise carrying a tomahawk-style tool to break a hole through the canopy. Others believe that if the plane flips, the impact will shatter the canopy and automatically create a way out.

Well, now I can tell you from experience that even if the canopy shatters, the pieces will not necessarily come apart. The broken pieces of my canopy were still in place, and they were hard to separate. A tool for knocking those pieces out would have been helpful. Gail and I believe it took between twenty and thirty minutes for both of us to finally get out, even with help from Bob, our Good Samaritan who was working at the airport.

Most Pilots are Sympathetic to Pilots Who Crash (Up to a Point)

I believe most pilots, when they first hear of an aviation accident, react by trying to insulate themselves from their own fears. How? By telling themselves that they are probably a better pilot than the poor fellow who just "bought the farm"—or at least a smarter pilot who wouldn't have taken the same risks. This is a similar mindset to that of self-confident young soldiers who, upon being told that roughly two thirds of them will not survive their next mission, all look pityingly to their left and to their right, thinking about how much they're going to miss both those guys.

In our more lucid moments, we know that bad things can, and sometimes do, happen to all of us. We say things like, "There, but for the grace of God, go I." And in one area of our brain we believe that. However, in another area of that same brain, we try to exercise some semblance of self-preservation, assuring ourselves that we would have handled the situation differently—this is human nature.

Mac McClellan, in the March 2014 issue of EAA's *Sport Aviation* magazine, wrote an article entitled, "Mistakes Will Be Made." I thought it provided some insight. He said,

> I have never liked the term "pilot error" as an explanation of an accident. The term is usually misleading and is essentially useless as a guide to improving safety. When "pilot error" is blamed for an accident it implies that other pilots are somehow perfect...The "pilot error" accident explanation is, in an odd way, flattering to

> those of us who fly. It implies that being a pilot demands a level of perfection only a few humans can attain, and those who somehow made it to the cockpit but were not really up to snuff made errors that did them in. The rest of us who haven't made errors yet clearly have the right stuff.

Seeing Your Plane Upside Down, After Working on It for Over 1,800 Hours, is Depressing

The word "depressing" does not even begin to describe the feeling. I thought of using "disheartening," "discouraging," or maybe just "the pit of despair," but no words seemed adequate.

Initially there was too much to be concerned about physically to think clearly about what had happened to the plane. Later on is when I was miserable, as I talked by phone to the guys in Maryland who were repairing the plane. It was tough hearing about the particular part they happened to be working on. At that point I was still not driving and had way too much time on my hands. I would think about the hours spent poring over the plans, and researching other builders' websites—trying to uncover any valuable tidbits or tricks on how to make something better. I enjoyed every stage of the building process, and looked forward to finally putting my hands on the materials for the actual construction.

The canopy had been a particularly challenging segment of the project: I had to wrestle the flimsy metal frame into proper configuration, so that it fit snugly onto the fuselage; attach the proper bracing to secure the metal frame; prime and paint the frame; cut, trim, and secure the plastic canopy to the metal frame without cracking it; fiberglass the canopy to the metal frame and make it look seamless; attach the fasteners and latches; finish painting the entire canopy; and connect the finished canopy to the fuselage.

This process took almost three months and involved over 160 hours of tedious work. I was proud of the finished product, and even now, as I sit at my desk and look at the pictures of that shattered canopy, I'm a little sad. The guys who repaired the plane did a great job, and overall I'm pleased, but I've got to be honest—my canopy was better.

The guys from Royal Aircraft in Hagerstown, Maryland, and me on the day they brought my plane back to W24. Tom Young is on the left and Bob Calo is in the middle. Just out of the picture is Bob's RV-7A that he had completed a year or two earlier.

A Five-Point Harness Trumps a Four-Point Harness

Until the unthinkable happens, it's hard to appreciate how important the lap belt is. The shoulder belts keep you from going forward in an accident, but the lap belt keeps your butt in the seat and your head from going through the canopy. Further, I read that the fifth belt—or crotch belt, if you prefer—is intended to keep you from sliding under the other belts and ending up below the instrument panel. That made sense, but I didn't think much about any other possible advantages of that extra little belt.

Then, when I posted my story on Vansairforce.net, a lot of other RV pilots responded with some sage safety advice. One of them explained that the fifth belt holds the lap belt down on the lap and enables you to really tighten the shoulder belts without having the lap belt lift up. That makes sense too.

Another RV builder, Larry Larson, wrote, "I second the five-point harness and the need to keep it tight. I drove race cars a bit and it's amazing how much you can torque them down after just a few minutes. The officials used to brief us, if you can still take a breath, the belt's not tight enough. I got used to pulling them tighter every yellow flag or pit stop." Sounds like good advice. I'm not saying I'll be keeping my belts that tight all through every flight, but for takeoffs and landings I guarantee they'll be pulled tight from now on.

I appreciate everyone who took the time to make a comment or offer a suggestion on that website. There was so much good advice that I'm certain anyone who took the time to read the thread would have benefited.

Good Insurance Helps to Relieve Some Stress

CJ, my older son, is the insurance guru in our family. He graduated from Temple University in 2005 with a degree in risk management and insurance. Who even knew there was such a degree? I didn't, until the day he called me near the end of his freshman year and said he had been invited to focus his curriculum in this new direction. At the time he was a declared business major with good grades. Apparently you have to be invited to join the insurance degree program, and he had been deemed worthy.

Neither of us knew much about the insurance profession at the time, but after a little investigation into some of the potential opportunities, he decided to give it a try. The school's program was ranked third in the nation and had an outstanding reputation. He figured if he didn't like it after a semester, he could always go back to a regular business degree—but he loved it and ended up graduating with honors. He stayed in Philadelphia after graduation and worked for a large insurance company for three or four years. Then I think the small-town boy got tired of the big city, and he came back to little Lynchburg, where he started his own independent agency.

I've recapped that bit of "Hagerty history" just to let you know that I have my own in-house, bona fide insurance professional. In fact, he had looked into writing the insurance for the plane himself, but decided that another source with access to more subject-specific markets would be a better choice.

I don't mind telling you the name of the company that we eventually chose, either, because I was more than pleased with their coverage and service. NationAir Aviation Insurance proved to be an excellent choice. They not only covered the plane at its declared value, but they included some extras in the policy that proved very helpful—a clause that paid for the plane's transport to where repair work could be done; hangar coverage; and $5,000 per person in medical coverage (whether or not other medical coverage was already in place).

I'm sure there are several other clauses in the policy that I'm not even aware of. But then again, I'm not the knowledgeable one. If you want to know all the details of my policy, you'll have to talk to our family's "insurance expert."

The FAA and Reexamination

The letter began: "Dear Mr. Hagerty: Investigation of the accident that occurred on June 15, 2013, at the Altoona–Blair County airport involving you as pilot in command of N954CH, gives reason to believe that a reexamination of your airman competency is necessary under Title 49 of the United States Code (49 U.S.C.)section 44709." This is the dreaded "Form 709" notice that I had only heard about before.

The letter went on to say, "Therefore, we request that you visit or telephone this office no later than 10 days from receipt of this letter to arrange for that reexamination. The reexamination will consist of appropriate Private Pilot knowledge areas with emphasis on Area of Operation IV, Takeoffs, Landings and Go-Arounds." The letter was dated a full two months after the accident occurred and was sent from the Flight Standards District Office in Pittsburgh. Clearly, they expected me to respond quickly and make arrangements to accommodate their test as soon as possible. The problem was that I was still wearing a halo—hardly conducive to flying.

As soon as I received the letter I called the FSDO in Pittsburgh and explained my dilemma. I asked to speak with the person who had signed the letter, but he wasn't available. So instead I had the good fortune to speak with Wendy Grimm, the director of the office. She couldn't have been more understanding. We talked about my injuries and how they would prohibit me from flying for at least several months and possibly a year. She seemed genuinely interested in my recovery and said so repeatedly.

I told Wendy I would stay in touch with her office and made certain that I called or emailed every month to keep them apprised of my progress. I'm still making those contacts, and as I sit at my desk looking at their 709 letter, it reminds me that it's time to call again tomorrow. I'm anxious to complete the reexamination and get it behind me—it'll be one more way to put the whole accident in the past.

It's Normal to Replay the Accident Repeatedly in Your Head

I really struggled with "what ifs" in the first months after the accident, but now that I'm getting close to the one-year anniversary, it's not as much of a problem. I think the main reason is that I'm busy again, and I don't have all that mind-numbing down time—idle hands, Devil's workshop, that sort of thing.

Most of the "what if" scenarios, of course, centered on what caused the accident and what I could have done differently. These thoughts went through my head constantly, and I'm sure I drove Gail crazy when I voiced them. I drove myself nuts too. Overall, though, I think the process was helpful in determining what I could do to prevent future mistakes.

However, there were unproductive "what if" scenarios as well, and they focused on how the accident could have been worse, with outcomes like death, paralysis, and fire. I suppose such thoughts could be normal, but I don't see how they could be helpful. The results of such negative thinking could only be anxiety, inaction, and even panic. Fortunately, those feelings lasted only a short time. I never dreamt about the accident, and I'm grateful for that.

It seemed as though almost everyone I talked with after the accident asked the same question—"Would I ever fly again?" I guess they were wondering if the unproductive "what if" thoughts were winning the battle in my head. I told them I'd have to wait until I was able to go up and then see how I felt. I didn't want to reply casually, because the accident had been traumatic enough to make me ask the same question. My brother Dan said that I was too dumb to know when to be cautious. He may be right, but I've always enjoyed flying, and I liked having my own plane, so I'll withhold a decision until I see what that next landing feels like.

Life is Surreal When You're Lying on the Grass Waiting for an Ambulance

How many thoughts would be going through your head if you were lying on the grass, with your wife, beside a plane that you had just wrecked? I had quite a few. *Is that gas? We need to get further from the plane. What is crawling on me? I hope Gail's all right. My poor parents. How bad's the plane? Where's my wallet? I worked on that plane forever. What did I do wrong? What will insurance cover? I can't fix it myself. How strong was that wind? My neck hurts. I wonder if my hand's going to work again. I really messed up. Who's going to move the plane? What about my appointments? What will I tell people? What will my pilot buddies think?*

These thoughts and more tumbled over and over in my head. And that nightmare I sometimes had as a kid—the one where I desperately tried to run away from monsters but instead kept stumbling and couldn't get up—was now reality. Just as in my dream, I wanted to escape from something terrible, but my body refused to cooperate.

Fortunately, we didn't have to lie there very long before the ambulances arrived and everything was in the hands of the EMTs. But for several surreal minutes Gail and I lay painfully on the damp grass, with little green bugs hopping all over us, feeling the heat of the June sun on our faces and listening to the wail of approaching sirens.

Eleven

Borrowed Insights on Hospitals

Everything's a Blur in the ER

THAT SEEMS LIKE AN OBVIOUS STATEMENT—AT LEAST NOW THAT I'm looking back it does. But at the time I'd never been brought to an emergency room in the back of a speeding ambulance complete with flashing lights and blaring sirens. Everything happened so fast that it was difficult to process it all.

The accident happened at about 1:20 p.m., and the ambulances got on site around 2:00 p.m. Between 3:00 and 3:30 p.m. we arrived at the hospital, and once inside the emergency room I lost all reference to time: I couldn't see a clock, I didn't have my phone (someone had taken it), and there were no windows. The only point of clarity I can remember was a phone call I made to the company that handled all my business appointments.

After that call everything was a haze of x-rays, CT scans, MRIs, and anxious inquiries about Gail's condition. This haze was compounded by the fact that the adrenaline and initial numbness of the accident had worn off and I was in quite a bit of pain.

Making the confusion worse was the inability to make decisions. I didn't know the full extent of my injuries and certainly didn't know how long the healing process was going to take. Would I be away from work for a week, a month, or a year? What would I be able to do (or not do) during recovery? What about driving? Will the injuries be permanent?

If you're a control freak like me (there, I admitted it, Gail!), part of the frustration is that you're unable to answer your own questions. Uncertainty, confusion, and helplessness govern the future as you lie waiting for answers.

Halo = Claustrophobia and Panic

For fifteen years, from 1988 until 2003, I owned a construction company that built in-ground swimming pools. Along with new construction, we also did repair work on existing pools. Although never as much fun as new construction, this work—fixing broken pipes, replacing liners, and doing general repairs—was nevertheless an important part of the business. Sometimes we had to tunnel under a concrete deck to reach a pipe that needed to be fixed. We usually would only tunnel three or four feet, and on anything that required more tunneling than that, we simply cut a hole in the deck and dug straight down to the problem.

Either way, this was never an easy job—not so much because of the hard digging, but because once the broken pipe was within reach, you had to twist and contort yourself into the narrow hole to make the repairs. If you had cut the concrete and were looking down at the pipe, you would have to hang upside down in the hole—not easy. I usually preferred tunneling. That way I could position myself horizontally and be a bit more comfortable...or at least not be hanging upside down.

On one job a couple of the guys dug the tunnel and then ran out of time before they were able to do the repair. The next day those men had to be somewhere else in the morning, so I decided to go over and fix the problem on my own. I figured I could fix the pipe and fill the hole within a few hours.

Now, these tunnels are only a couple of feet deep, and the concrete pool deck is directly overhead, so there is no danger of the dirt collapsing. They're still tunnels, though, so they are usually narrow, always dark, and smell like worms. You lower yourself head first into the hole, with a lot of bending and twisting. Then you try to squirm into a horizontal position with your feet elevated above your head.

Are you starting to get the picture...Is it hard to get your breath yet? Usually I was fine, but this time I turned too quickly to reposition myself, and suddenly my shoulders were stuck in the dirt walls of the tunnel. I couldn't move. *Oh, no. This isn't good!*

Because I was by myself, I panicked. My heart rate shot up, my breathing became rapid and shallow, and the more I struggled, the tighter I became wedged. It took all the willpower I could muster to calm down, breathe deeply, and slowly wriggle my shoulders free. That was my worst claustrophobic experience ever.

So when the sedation wore off in that Pennsylvania hospital and I felt the full effect of having a halo on, my mind raced back to that tunnel. This was a different kind of claustrophobia, and though I was upright and above ground this time, the panic caused by the inability to move my head was just as real.

News Flash: Inserting Screws Into Your Skull Does Hurt

Sometimes I possess an acute sense of the obvious. I guess it goes without saying that if you take a sharply pointed screw and twist it into your head, it's going to hurt. But the worst part is not when the pointy piece of metal pierces the skin; it's when the skin is crushed between the screw and your skull. There's a crunching sensation as the screw is tightened, and it's an odd, unpleasant feeling.

In the *Wheeless' Textbook of Orthopaedics* doctors are told how to install halo screws (or "pins"):

- once the pin positions are selected, the pins are inserted;
- it is not necessary to incise the skin with a scalpel, and posteriorly it is not necessary to shave the patient's hair;
- have patient close eyes during pin insertion;
- each pin should be placed until they just touch the skin;
- one front pin and the diagonally opposite back pin are tightened to maximum finger tension;
- other pins are likewise tightened;
- torque screw driver is then used to tighten the pins, again tightening them in pairs first;
- consider 6- to 8 in-lbs of tightness (10 in-lbs will begin to pass through the outer table);
- unequal tension should not be used, as the halo will migrate in the direction of the pin of least tension.

I especially like the third directive where the doctor is instructed to "have patient close eyes." Good advice.

Apart from the physical pain of having four pointy screws screwed into your skull, followed by intense pressure, there are a number of other ways the halo device can cause pain and discomfort. Again, *Wheeless' Textbook of Orthopaedics* has this to say:

> The medical records of 179 patients were reviewed to identify complications related to the use of the halo external skeletal-fixation device. The complications that were identified included pin-loosening in 36 per cent of the patients, pin-site infection in 20 per cent, pressure sores under either a plastic vest or a plaster cast in 11 per cent, nerve injury in 2 per cent, dural penetration in 1 per cent, dysphagia in 2 per cent, cosmetically disfiguring scars in 9 per cent, and severe pin discomfort in 18 per cent. One hundred and eighty (25 per cent) of the 716 pins used had become loose at least once, and an infection had developed at sixty-seven pin sites (9 per cent). Two thirds of the pins that were loose or associated with infection required change or removal. These complication rates, particularly of pin-loosening and infection, are exceedingly high. Attention to details in pin application, pin maintenance, and proper pin-site care may minimize the number of complications.

I'm thankful for modern medicine, but as I said several times during my three months of wearing a halo, *I would never wish the experience on anyone.*

The Halo Weighs 7.2 Pounds, and It Looks Strange Hanging From Your Head

Just as a point of reference, a gallon of milk weighs 8.35 lbs. That's a fair amount of weight to have hanging from screws fastened into your skull. The ring encircling your head, and the screws going through the ring and into your head, wouldn't be of much benefit unless they were securely attached to a hard plastic vest that fits over your torso. This vest keeps the neck from moving.

Unfortunately, although the vest may appear to be resting on your shoulders, at times almost all the weight of the device is suspended from the screws. At other times, the vest is squeezing your body and supporting the weight of the contraption. The good news is that whether the weight of the halo is supported by the screws or by the plastic vest, there are no nerve endings in your skull. This means that once the screws are in, they don't hurt—you still feel pressure, but that's about all.

I always thought the halo looked especially strange and uncomfortable when I was lying down. Usually I would lie on my back, and the two screws at the rear would be the only things supporting the weight of my entire head. How much does a normal adult male head weigh, anyway? According to a quick Google search, eight to twelve pounds, without hair, is normal. I weigh less than 170 pounds, so my head would probably be closer to the eight- or nine-pound size. Regardless, it looked peculiar when two pointy screws were the only things supporting it.

For some reason, when I saw myself lying down, I would think of severed heads on pikes (I've seen one too many "Braveheart"-type movies, I guess), or those freaky people on the Discovery Channel who like to suspend their bodies from metal hooks. One guy actually suspended himself from a metal framework on the back of a flatbed truck and had his friend drive him around town. I think they were advertising their tattoo/piercing business in Las Vegas.

I know I'm just rambling, but the point is that an installed halo looks strange because it *is* strange. We don't normally put screws in our heads and then suspend several pounds from them. You know, here's something I hadn't thought of before; I still have my halo, and I've always liked to travel. Maybe I need to figure a way to take this show on the road...Anybody have a flatbed truck?

Nighttime is the Worst Time in a Hospital

If you've ever spent a few days in the hospital, I won't have to convince you that this is a true statement. You're already nodding in agreement. The days are bad enough, but I think the nights are worse because of two things—despondency and loneliness. It's hard to keep your spirits up when you're by yourself.

For most of us, the world is a foreign place at 3:00 a.m. Nothing feels normal at that time, and our bodies tell us we should be sleeping soundly somewhere that is comfortable and preferably familiar. A hospital bed is neither. Throw in an unpleasant concoction of pain, anxiety, drugs, light, noise, and unusual smells, and you have the makings of one long, unpleasant night. While the circumstances may be similar during the day, if you are fortunate enough to have visitors, you're at least distracted for awhile.

Gail was often surprised when she came to the hospital—usually around 10:00 a.m.—to spend the day with me. She would walk in, asking how my night had gone, and I would tell her about one of the nurses whose daughter just had her tenth birthday. Or about an orderly whose father finally had to be put into a home because his dementia had gotten much worse. Or about another nurse who had just moved back to the area after living in Louisiana for the past five years, and who had recently broken up with her boyfriend.

"How do you know all these things?" she would ask, "you're beginning to sound like me." Gail has always talked to everyone, curious to learn as much about them as time allowed. One of my sayings about her is that "she's never met a stranger, only friends she doesn't know yet." I, on the other hand, was just the opposite. Always focused on a job, an object, or a deadline, I seldom took the time to learn about people. Now, however, as I lay in a strange place, watching the red numbers on the digital clock click past 3:00 a.m., I was learning something new: If I asked a lot of questions, my late-night caretakers would stay longer and talk with me.

Having Friends Who are Medical Professionals is Invaluable

Having an inside contact is always a good thing, whether you're visiting a foreign country, betting on horses, or experiencing an extended stay at a local hospital. In my case, the local hospital was not back in Lynchburg, but it *was* in my parents' home town, and they had lived there all their lives. Between them and my brother Dan, they know a lot of people.

One of our first contacts was a nurse who met Gail and me when we were brought into the ER. Amanda Burke is my niece's husband's sister. I had met Amanda at least once or twice before, but in the hospital I was too out of it to remember her. She was the one who kept the family informed about our condition and what was being done for us on the other side of the curtains.

Tammy Wills and her husband, Doug, attend the same church as my parents and have known them for a long time. Tammy has been an operating room nurse for more than ten years. She knows the inside scoop on most of the local doctors—which ones you want to operate on you and which you don't. The Willses' personal visits, along with Tammy's advice on the fusion I had to have done, were a big help.

Dr. Jack Rocco and his wife Kari Ann have two of the cutest kids in the world. Sophia is eight years old and her brother James is six. My mother first met the Roccos when Jack did a knee replacement for my father; Sophia was just a baby then. Both Jack and Kari Ann's parents live out of state, so when Mom saw Sophia, she instantly decided this baby girl needed an additional grandmother. Kari Ann was a little less enthusiastic at first, but as she got to know my mother, they quickly became friends.

Jack was not only there from the beginning to comfort Mom and Dad, but months later when things weren't looking good and another operation was needed, he helped me make some difficult decisions. He was also responsible for getting Gail back in for more x-rays after the ER initially said they had found everything that was wrong—she had two undetected cracked ribs. Our heartfelt thanks go out to all three of these medical professionals and friends.

Hospital Toothpaste, Preparation H, and Pain Pills…Not a Good Combination

What sort of twisted, devious monster would ever do something like this? The caps are identical, the length and diameter of each tube is the same, and the colors, although slightly different, are much too similar. I ask you again, from what sort of sinister mind does such malevolence emanate?

It was just my second day in SPCU, and I was still struggling to get out of bed on my own and walk twenty or thirty feet without falling. But at least it was progress, and I was glad for it. I was also glad to be able to go into the bathroom by myself. I was still supposed to have an orderly or nurse help me when I walked, but at least they would leave me to my own devices and close the door once I reached the bathroom. This was real freedom!

Along with this independence came the ability to brush my teeth. You don't realize how much you miss brushing your teeth until you haven't done it for three or four days. Another condition I was able to deal with on my own now was the indelicate problem of hemorrhoids. Maybe the "pucker factor" at the time of the crash was more severe than I'd realized, but this malady had now become personal.

You've got to remember that although I may have been able to stand upright, I was far from being lucid at this point. I was still taking a strong painkiller; my right hand wasn't working very well; and having a halo on in a tiny half-bathroom didn't leave much room for turning and maneuvering. I'm saying all this now, just to let you know it was an honest mistake—anyone could have done it. And while I may not know what Preparation H tastes like, I can assure you that toothpaste does burn!

Ambulance Gurneys are Really, Really Uncomfortable

Have you ever ridden in the back of an ambulance, strapped to a gurney? I hadn't either. These wheeled cots are a valuable tool. They are lightweight, yet rugged and strong; they can be rolled over uneven terrain; and the collapsible legs make it easy to get the patient up and into the ambulance. They really are hardworking pieces of medical equipment. However, I can attest that they become miserably uncomfortable after a very short time.

In a nutshell, the padding is thin and hard and not very wide. And then, to top it off, the ambulances that carry these gurneys have stiff suspension and ride like a rock wagon. Granted, I was extra sensitive because of the pain from my injuries, but I felt every bump and divot in the road.

Fortunately, long-distance trips are not usually what these vehicles are used for. When I rode in the one that picked Gail and me up after the accident, I didn't complain about how stiff the ride was or how uncomfortable the gurney was because there were too many other things happening. So don't get me wrong, these are great pieces of equipment for doing what they do best—carrying a bunch of heavy medical tools, while also picking up injured people and getting them quickly to a hospital.

But if you ever have to travel several hours in one, you might want to ask more questions than I did and make certain an ambulance is your only option. Because, believe me, you won't enjoy the ride.

Swallowing is Scary When the Halo is First Put On

I realize that some of the information in this book is subject-specific and applicable to only a small minority of people—namely, those unfortunate enough to wear a halo. However, I tell these stories for three reasons: (a) The experience was intense and affected my life significantly; (b) the unique nature of this medical device attracts attention, and information about it could be universally interesting; and (c) this information might be beneficial to someone else who has to wear a halo.

I've already mentioned this earlier, but try swallowing without tilting your head just a little bit. It can be done with practice, but the more normal process seems to involve moving your head back slightly. According to a journal article from the Palo Alto Medical Foundation, "Swallowing involves many nerves and about fifty muscles, because moving food into the stomach is a complicated task." The article went on to list fifteen conditions that can cause problems, with head and neck injuries at the top of the list.

So trying to swallow anything scared me. Because of the trauma, my weakened condition, and the halo, I knew I was going to choke, and if I did, the nurses would never get the vest off in time to perform the Heimlich maneuver. And if they somehow did get the vest off, they would probably sever my spinal cord by performing such a violent procedure on someone with an unsupported broken neck. It looked like a vicious cycle and an uncomfortable way to die.

Obviously my fears were not unfounded. It may have been closer to four or five weeks before I even started to feel comfortable with swallowing. I know that thoughts of choking were always in the back of my mind, and I learned to take small bites, chew thoroughly, and swallow everything from water to steak with caution.

Loosening the First Screw of the Halo is Memorable

Removing the halo was done without sedation, and when the first screw was loosened, the sensation was not what I expected. I thought the skin around the screws might have become partially adhered to each screw, and that there would be a stinging or burning feeling as the two were pulled apart.

That's not what happened. Instead, there was such intense pressure on my entire head that I thought Dr. Gill was tightening the screw instead of loosening it.

Whoa, are you going in the right direction? He assured me he was, and said that the screw was already out. I told him about the pressure, and he promised me that was normal. *How about a little warning next time* is what I thought but didn't say.

The remaining three screws were out in a matter of minutes, and then the entire vest along with the supporting carbon rods was removed. The feeling of intense pressure remained for about thirty minutes and then slowly eased. The feeling of elation, however, was more powerful than the pain. It was hard to believe I had actually grown accustomed to such restrictions and discomfort.

Now that it wasn't a part of me anymore and I could sit on the bed and look at it from a detached perspective (literally), I threatened to take it home and mount it on the wall like a trophy set of deer antlers.

For some reason, Gail objected.

Damage to the C6/C7 Vertebrae Can Affect the Right Hand

When the accident first happened, my right hand didn't work at all. That only lasted a few days, though, and after seven or eight weeks my grip had returned to almost normal. Unfortunately, there remained a numb, burning sensation that I likened to sticking my hand in a bucket of ice water. It's a dull ache throughout the hand combined with a pricking sensation in the fingers. It's unpleasant, but it's also tolerable; if I become focused on a task, I actually don't notice the pain for awhile. At night I wear a thin cloth glove that keeps the fingers from touching and helps me sleep.

Apparently the nerves that come from the spinal cord and go to the fingers of the right hand begin their journey by going through the spinal column at the point of the C6/C7 vertebrae—the exact two vertebrae I had to have fused together. This is the same area of the neck where I may have lost some spinal fluid.

I tried taking Neurontin for several months, starting about a week after the accident, but it didn't seem to help very much. I also didn't like the way it made me feel. Dr. Gill talked about switching to Lyrica, but first I decided to see how I felt taking nothing. So far I've opted to put up with the discomfort rather than deal with the side effects of the medicine.

In early May 2014, I had an EMG test done by Dr. Joyner's office in Lynchburg. This test involved sending electricity through the hand and arm to determine the levels of conductivity in the nerves. An assistant performed this part of the procedure, and it lasted for almost an hour. She had to test both arms and hands in order to establish a baseline in the good (left) hand. By the time we were nearing the end of the test, I promised her I would divulge any information she wanted, including classified government secrets, if she would only stop shocking me. She assured me that by this point in the interrogation—uh, I mean "test"—all of her patients were willing to do just about anything she asked.

After the assistant was finished, Dr. Joyner came in for his portion of the procedure. This involved inserting a thin metal probe with a wire attached into various parts of my neck, arm, and hand. The probe was just a little thicker than a human hair and it really wasn't too painful, until he stuck it into the palm of my hand. Fortunately, we didn't have to do both hands for this part of the test.

I have an appointment to see Dr. Gill in a week, and he's supposed to explain the results of the test. He'll tell me if anything can be done surgically to relieve the pain in my hand…I hope I'll have some options.

Part of Your Head Will Be Numb If a Halo Screw Hits a Nerve

Specifically in my case, it was the right rear quadrant of my head. Apparently there is a fairly significant nerve that goes up that side of the head, and I was unlucky enough to have the screw hit it. Numbness resulted, and a section of skin became sensitive to touch. Haircuts became unpleasant. I don't know if there are other main nerves that could be affected by one of the other screws, but for me the problem was only in that right rear area.

This problem lasted the entire three months the halo was on and then for about nine months after it was removed. Thankfully, the sensation has almost disappeared, and it's much easier now to laugh with my niece Alesha—the witty college girl—when she uses the word "numbskull."

Considering all the complications that often occur with those screws, I was fortunate. If you remember some of those statistics from *Wheeless' Textbook of Orthopaedics*, thirty-six percent of patients have screw-loosening problems, twenty percent get infections at the site of the screw, and nine percent end up with cosmetically disfiguring scars from the screws. Gail was diligent about cleaning the site of my four screws, and I was lucky to avoid these types of complications.

The father of a business acquaintance, however, was not so fortunate. Judy Frantz has been a real estate agent in our town for almost twenty years, and her husband is a heart and lung surgeon. I've known Judy for almost as long as she's been a realtor. When I was able to return to work and saw her for the first time in over ten months, we talked a few minutes about my accident, and then she told me about her father.

John Lee is now ninety-one years old, and he broke his neck for the first time in 1996. He was seventy-three years old then, and he had breaks in the C1/C2 area of his neck. I can't imagine how a person that age could endure wearing a halo, but that's what he did for three long months. He also ended up getting an infection at one of the screw sites.

As difficult as that was, however, his story got worse. Fourteen years later, he slipped while coming down a ladder and broke his neck again. This time he broke it in the C5/C6 area, and at the age of eighty-seven, he—unbelievably—had to wear the halo a second time for another three months. I don't think I could do that. Another thing he told me, when I called one day, was that the screws were bigger on the first halo and caused considerable scarring. He has assured me that the equipment today is much better than it was eighteen years ago.

John and I have never met in person, but I can tell you something for a fact—mentally and physically, this is a very tough man. I for one am never going to ask him what in the world he was doing climbing ladders at the age of eighty-seven.

Twelve

Borrowed Insights on Recovery

Is a Rehabilitation Center Necessary? (Short Answer: Yes)

WHEN WE RETURNED TO VIRGINIA AFTER THE ACCIDENT, GAIL thought I might have done just as well if I had bypassed the Acute Rehabilitation Center and gone directly home. I disagreed for the following reasons:

- I was completely exhausted from the painful ambulance ride and had to have help with everything for a day or two.
- The transition back to real food was rocky; I had problems with nausea, so choking was a real concern.
- A doctor checked on me each morning and monitored the problem with my right hand, prescribing something for it after the first day.
- The center's evaluation of my strength and abilities gave me a baseline from which to measure progress.

- The exercises were specific to my needs and got my rehab started in the right direction.
- The safety information and advice the staff provided was invaluable when I did return home.

And last (but not least), Gail had been gone from home for almost a week and still had her own injuries to deal with. My being at the rehab center gave her a chance to rest and adjust to being home before having to deal with my needs.

People Stare at You but Rarely Speak When You Have a Halo On

Excluding myself, I have only seen one other person wearing a halo--ever. It was about ten years ago, and a young man who was a close friend of my sons was getting married. Gideon had grown up with our family and played baseball with CJ from Little League through American Legion ball. Now CJ was going to be his best man, and we were all going to the wedding.

Gideon's prospective father-in-law was involved in a car wreck a couple of months before the wedding, and he had a halo on to immobilize his broken neck. He got around great—he even did some slow dance steps—but he did look odd. The device completely immobilizes your head and neck. You look like something out of a zombie movie as you stiffly walk around, turning and bending at the waist every time you need to see in a different direction.

And that's just the way *you* look and move. What about the way the device looks? Any piece of equipment that is attached to your body by four screws fastened into your head is going to appear bizarre. It's also going to look painful, and sensitive people are visibly squeamish when they first see you.

Gail had to wear a Miami J collar for a few months after the accident, while I was also in my halo, and when we were out together in public the double-takes were not well hidden. Some people would ask questions or make comments, but almost always these were directed to Gail and not to me. Later on, after my second surgery, I had to wear a Miami J for about three months. Then people would talk to me—I guess I had become more approachable and less scary.

I'm trying to remember if I ever spoke with Gideon's father-in-law at the wedding. I don't think I did. I didn't know him, we were not seated at the same table, and he always seemed to be talking to someone else. At least those are the best excuses I can come up with right now. To be honest, at the time I just didn't know what to say to someone who looked that strange.

Halos Make It Hard to Sleep, Especially For the First Four Weeks

Sleep in the hospital was almost unattainable—I eventually just passed out for an hour or less. Sleeping in the rehab center was a step up, with perhaps three hours of rest at a time. But it wasn't until I got home that I was able to experiment with a beanbag chair.

CJ was the first to search the internet to see if anyone else with a halo experience had devised a way to make sleeping more tolerable. I heard stories about those who never even tried to sleep in a bed during their entire experience of wearing the device. Instead, they would "sleep"—a relative term—in a semi-reclined position in their favorite chair. I can understand that. Just getting up and down was difficult enough, but trying to roll from one side to the other during the night was unpleasant enough to make you dread lying down.

Anyway, CJ found information about one sufferer who had taken a small cloth-covered bean bag chair (vinyl won't work) and emptied about half of the Styrofoam "beans." This created extra squishiness in the chair, allowing it to mold itself around the framework of the halo. When I tested this idea, I found that by placing my head on the bag and wiggling back and forth, I could work the frame of the halo down into the bag. The beans would then squish up around the frame and provide a measure of support for my head. This was preferable at first to just having my head held up by two screws.

After four weeks I continued to use the bag, but most of the time it was just like any other pillow, and I didn't worry about staying squished down into the thing. I guess I had gotten used to the pressure created by the screws. That—and the fact that I took two pain pills and a muscle relaxant—would provide around four hours of sleep. Then I would wake up, take another pain pill, and sleep for two more hours. Adaptation and medication at their finest, working hand in hand.

I Missed the Little Things

Life, when going smoothly, is a harmonious compilation of numerous little things. Yes, the big events, the big places, the big things are all nice, but the everyday activities and things we take for granted are what we really miss when our circumstances take a turn for the worse.

Think of all the things that go into having just a good old regular work day…let's say it's a Tuesday. Hopefully you slept well on a bed that was comfortable, in a place that was dry, and not too hot or too cold. Then you got up, turned on the lights, and enjoyed the many benefits of running water—probably both hot and cold (you lucky dog). Maybe you even had clean clothes to put on before you made your way—by yourself, with your own strength—to another room where there was food to eat. I could go on and on, but you get the point. Every day is full of a hundred good things we take for granted and that we enjoy far more than appreciate.

Taking a shower was one of those things. I've seldom been a jump-in, jump-out type of person; I've always taken long, hot showers. But until I broke my neck, I never fully appreciated this small daily luxury. Yes, I could sit in a shallow tub of water and get clean, and yes, Gail was a good helper. We even worked out a system where I would lower my head over the edge of the tub and she could wash my hair (fortunately I have very short hair). But none of this provided the all-over cleanliness and soothing steaminess of a long, hot shower.

In the Summer You Sweat a Lot When Wearing a Halo

July, August, and September in Virginia are especially brutal months to be outfitted with a halo. Why? Because it's hot and humid, and part of the halo is a thick, fluffy, wool vest wrapped around the torso. Almost anything you do, even in your air-conditioned home, is going to make you sweat. If you're smart, you won't even think about going outside.

On the rare times that I walked out of the house to get the mail—a round trip of about 400 feet—I would have to come back in immediately and change the modified T-shirt that I wore under the vest. That T-shirt trick and copious amounts of cornstarch were the two things that got me through the summer. I forget if we learned about cornstarch on the internet or from the halo literature we received from the doctor. Baby powder will clump up on the wool fibers, so you definitely don't want to use that. Clumpy wool fibers act like sandpaper and are very hard on the skin.

At first the whole sweat issue isn't a problem because you're not able to do much of anything except lie around. It's later, when you start to feel better and get some of your strength back, that you run the risk of hurting yourself. Can you imagine how miserable it would be to get a severe rash or sores under a hot, plastic breastplate that you're not able to remove?

I did hurt myself once, about six weeks after the accident. I had a small commercial building that needed some renovations before a new tenant was scheduled to move in during August. I had arranged for another contractor to do the work, and now all that remained were a few loose ends and some cleanup. My sister-in-law, Vickie, and her son, Caleb, had been helping us for the past few weeks, and it was Caleb who drove me to the building.

There I proceeded to do more than I should have. Granted, it wasn't much, but for me it was still too much, and I paid the price. The red rash was painful, and the verbal chastisement from Gail sounded something like, "Just how dumb are you, anyway?" I'm grateful that in addition to this well-deserved tongue-lashing, she also found the right products to ease my suffering and prevent the rash from becoming worse.

Life Changes Tremendously When You Can't Drive

For some people, not being able to drive would just not be an issue. Maybe they live in a major metropolitan area with outstanding public transit, and owning a car is more of a hassle than a necessity. Not so for me. I did live in Pittsburgh during graduate school, but even there my old Chevy Nova was a necessary evil.

Besides, for as long as I can remember, I've always liked anything with wheels and a motor. My paternal grandparents had a riding lawn mower, and I would plead with them, when I was eight or nine years old, to let me put it in fourth gear so I could go fast down their long gravel driveway. When I was eleven, my friend George and I painted racing stripes on his sister's 1959 Chevy Impala—yes, we did have her permission. When I was fourteen, my friend Tom "borrowed" his father's truck so we could go joyriding. He was on his way to pick me up when he took a corner too fast and ended up in the ditch—no, we did not have his dad's permission. And at fifteen I bought my first car, so I could work on it for a year before I turned sixteen.

Cars represent freedom to all age groups, from sixteen to eighty-six and beyond (if you can get away with it). Gail and I live in a rural part of central Virginia where the closest country store/gas station is about seven miles away. She drives forty-five to fifty minutes, one way, to get to Roanoke for work, and I cover a lot of territory with my business. Obviously, there is no way we could live where we live and do what we do without our vehicles.

So to go from driving one day to not driving the next, and then to have this restriction imposed for five months, was anguish. Those of you who've had to wear ankle bracelets—you know who you are—understand what I'm talking about. Fortunately Caleb served as my chauffeur for a few weeks, and then right after he returned home, my dad was available to drive me around for awhile. However, after Dad went back to Pennsylvania, I was home alone for four more months. This experience gave me an entirely different level of empathy for anyone who loses the ability to drive.

When You Can't Bend Your Neck and Look Down, It's Hard to Aim

The bathroom had become an obstacle course, a several-times-daily reminder that life was now more difficult than it had ever been before. Washing my face wasn't too bad, except now I had to work around carbon rods, a thick plastic ring, and four titanium screws. Brushing my teeth was still basically the same—once I finally found the toothpaste in the cabinet drawer—but rinsing and spitting were a problem.

Unlike both my grandmothers, who always had little disposable cups sitting on each bathroom sink, we are the type of people who bend over and sip from the flowing stream of water (but never, ever, do we let our lips touch the spigot—those who do are just uncivilized). This sipping system was now impossible, and so I joined ranks with the millions of others who fill landfills every day with Dixie cups.

Let me back up now for a second. Why do you think it was hard to find toothpaste in the cabinet drawer? Because I wear trifocals, and all of you other old people who wear these stupid things know how we constantly tilt our heads to find that narrow part of the lens that enables us to focus. Now imagine wearing your glasses and not being able to adjust the angle of your head. Exactly...you understand my dilemma.

Taking a shower was the next bathroom challenge, and all I could do was stand and look longingly at the shower head. Getting clean had morphed into something that was both inefficient and unsatisfying. There's no comparison between the invigorating all-over cleaning power of a steamy hot shower and the lukewarm alternative—a tepid sponge bath in a shallow tub (this is the second time I've lamented my inability to shower…I must have missed this even more than I realized).

The last bathroom function is one I'll try to deal with delicately. For obvious reasons, if you're a guy, *you will have to sit down*. Standing and estimating trajectory and distance will not result in the desired outcome—or a happy wife. The next, and less obvious, problem is how to determine when toilet tissue has completed the task that toilet tissue was designed to do. Guesswork here is also unsatisfactory.

Let me give you a hint in case you're struggling to understand. When I was in Costa Rica and Chile, the public restrooms instructed you not to flush toilet paper. Instead, you were supposed to place the paper in a receptacle beside the toilet (yeah, that took some getting used to for me also). But the *concept* of that experience proved to be beneficial as I struggled to adapt everyday life to living with a halo.

After that amount of self-revelation and embarrassing candor, I certainly hope this information proves helpful to someone, someday.

Prescription Drugs Make You Tired and Dull

Ever looking for that silver lining, and not wanting to turn a bad accident into a collection of totally wasted months, I thought of several things I wanted to accomplish once I was back home. Unencumbered by a normal work schedule, I envisioned reading many books, completing some paperwork for Bedford County, and even organizing notes on a subject I considered writing about one day.

But alas, as the saying goes, "The best-laid plans of mice and men often go awry." John Steinbeck, in his 1937 novel entitled *Of Mice and Men,* is often given credit for this saying. However, it's actually an English paraphrase of a line in a Scots poem written by Robert Burns in 1785. Steinbeck just borrowed the phrase to use for the title of his book. I know that's probably more information than you wanted to know, but I thought it was interesting. And unfortunately, the saying does accurately describe what happened to my plans…they definitely went awry.

Because of my moderation when it comes to taking drugs, the pills that I took really worked well. I had hydrocodon-acetaminophen for pain; cyclobenzaprine as needed for muscle spasms; and gabapentin (Neurontin) for nerve pain in my right hand and arm. This pharmaceutical cocktail, although not much by many people's standards, was enough to keep me listless and lethargic from mid-June until early December. I was able to get through several books, but the other projects that I intended to work on just didn't happen.

After Six Months in a Halo and a Hard Collar, Your Neck Won't Move

Well, surprise—what did I expect? I had never been through this before, so I really didn't know what was going to happen. Of course I knew that everything would be tight and weak, but I was hoping—or was it wishful thinking?—that I'd be able to turn my head just a little bit after the collar came off. No such luck. Everything was locked up tight.

I had the hard collar off for almost two months before Dr. Gill gave me permission to begin an official rehab program. Unofficially, I had been doing gentle stretching and moving exercises to loosen the atrophied neck muscles, but it took the entire two months to even begin to loosen things up. Find an anatomical chart that shows all the body's muscle groups and you'll be amazed at the number of muscles from the chest, shoulders, and back that secure your head to the rest of your body.

When I began going to rehab in February 2013, I tried to hit it hard. I generally went two times a week for around an hour each time; I saw a massage therapist twice a week for half-hour sessions; and I did bending and stretching exercises at home for about thirty or forty minutes every day. In spite of all this, it didn't seem like I was making any progress. My neck would feel better for an hour after each session, but then it would tighten right back up again.

Ever so slowly, though, others began to notice a difference in how much I was turning my head. Jimmy Miller is a realtor who has some property of mine listed for sale, and we got together to talk right after I was able to resume driving. We then saw each other again almost three months later, and he told me he saw a considerable difference in the amount my head was able to turn. I really couldn't notice much improvement myself, but he assured me it was so, and his encouragement made me feel better.

I Thought Rehab Would be Easier Than It Actually Was

Don't ask me why I thought that. Maybe I was anxious to get back to some semblance of normalcy. Maybe I knew I needed to return to my business, because I was running out of money. Maybe I thought I was in fairly good condition for a guy in his late fifties. Or maybe at this point I just needed something—anything—to be easy.

Regardless of what I thought, I knew after the first few days that rehab was not going to be a cakewalk. I think the area that hurt the worst was the front of each shoulder, where the bones from the arm nestle into the shallow recess of the shoulder socket. I wasn't able to reach my arms above my head for a long time, and it was difficult to pull my arms into the sleeve of a jacket or shirt.

Richard, my rehabilitation expert, took some measurements and came to the conclusion that the angle at which the halo had kept my shoulders tilted forward, along with such a lengthy period of inactivity, is what was causing my discomfort. *Oh well, got to work with what you've got.* So I started with the simplest of exercises: shoulder shrugs, windmills (circles made with both arms straight out), stretching the neck from side to side, and a few other easy motions.

After several weeks the simple exercises that incorporated extremely light weights—can you believe, one pound—were slowly upgraded to more targeted movements with heavier weights. Progress was slow, but at least I was headed in the right direction.

Knowing that my C1 vertebrae had only knit partially kept me from being too aggressive initially with therapy.

Dr. Gill said we would wait six months and then take another CT scan in the hope that we would see a more solid bone structure. In the meantime, I was careful not to do anything that would damage any of his fine surgical work. Good neck mobility might not be a reality yet, but at least I had not been completely fused, and I was grateful.

Statistics Aren't Favorable When You Break Your Neck

After the accident, when I wasn't able to drive for five months or work for nine, I had plenty of time to look at online medical sites. What I learned about broken necks and cervical spine fractures was both fascinating and unnerving. Most injuries that involve the neck or cervical spine are the result of a violent collision that compresses the cervical spine against the shoulders.

People who participate in high-impact sports—such as diving, equestrian activities, football, gymnastics, skiing, hang gliding, and racing—are all at risk for cervical fractures. Motor vehicle accidents account for fifty percent of injuries; falls, twenty percent; sports-related activities, fifteen percent; and other high-velocity accidents, fifteen percent. The male-to-female ratio for those suffering such fractures is four to one, and eighty percent of accident victims are between the ages of eighteen and twenty-five.

There are seven vertebrae in the cervical spine, and most injuries occur at one of two levels. One third of neck injuries occur at the C2 level, and one half of such injuries occur at C6 or C7. Most of the fatal cervical spine injuries occur in the upper levels, either at C1 or C2. The late Christopher Reeve broke both C1 and C2 in the equestrian accident that left him a quadriplegic.

The online resource MD Guidelines (mdguidelines.com) estimates that there are about 11,000 spinal injuries in the United States each year. Approximately 6,000 of these injuries result in death and about 5,000 in quadriplegia. They say that "the overall incidence of cervical spinal fracture *without* spinal cord injury is three percent." Those aren't very good odds.

When the accident drove my head into the ground, I broke C1 in two places, C2 in one place, C6 in one place, and C7 in one place. There was some immediate damage to the spinal cord in the C6/C7 area—accompanied by some leaking of spinal fluid, and that's why my right hand wouldn't work. I'm very thankful that the use of my hand returned after a few weeks and that the only residual effect from the spinal cord damage is numbness and burning in that hand. It's irritating, and a constant problem, but it's also tolerable—and a whole lot better than the alternatives.

Thirteen

Borrowed Insights on Relationships

Things Would be Worse If You Did Not Have a Caring Spouse, Friend, or Caregiver

AT FIRST GLANCE, THIS IS A SELF-EVIDENT STATEMENT: IF YOU'RE unable to do certain things for yourself, you will need someone who is able and willing to help you. Without that help, daily life would be exceedingly difficult or even impossible. But the key word I meant to focus on is "caring." What if the person providing the assistance is resentful or angry…indifferent or calloused? Now your predicament just became worse.

Gail could not have taken better care of me during the four or five months that I was unable to care for myself. Both her physical support and her emotional support were invaluable, and it would have been much harder to make it through this dark time without her. As I sit at my desk writing this paragraph, it is one day after the celebration of our thirty-fourth wedding anniversary.

I can honestly say, and I'm sure Gail would agree, that this past year has been a good one for us. We've drawn closer together, and I made some changes that helped me focus less on the trivial things that can sometimes derail marriages and more on the long-range, positive facets of our relationship.

I'll never admit to being stubborn, though, because all it took for me to change was a hard blow to the head and a broken neck.

Be a Better Encourager

Big problems, little problems, we've all got them. And in typical male fashion, many of us ignore them and just keep soldiering on. Some of us also tend to ignore the problems our friends have—maybe we're too busy to invest time to talk, or maybe we're just uncomfortable talking about problems we happen to share.

I think the main reason I've not been good at encouraging my friends is that I've always liked to be busy—too busy. And I don't have a good sense of moderation when I get involved in something; I develop tunnel vision, and the task at hand is all I can focus on. There's probably a psychological term for this, but I don't know what it is. One thing I do know is that when I was the one down and needing some encouragement, I appreciated my friends and family who took the time to support me.

Sadly, most of the lessons I've learned have been learned the hard way. I wish I was wiser and able to put into practice the sage pieces of advice I've heard or read over the years. However, maybe there are some things that are impossible to relate to until they're experienced personally. It wasn't that I didn't want to encourage others; I just never thought about what it would be like to be idle, unable to work, and isolated in the house all day.

Now that I know how that feels, I have a greater sense of empathy. I can appreciate the struggles of older people and those with disabilities. And while none of us can experience and relate to everything—I don't know what combat's like, and I'll probably never live in a South American jungle—I do know how it feels to need encouragement.

Just this past year a friend went through a divorce, a contractor buddy of mine had a heart attack, another friend lost his mother, and a family member's physical condition continued to deteriorate. These things happen every day, but this time I made more phone calls, took the time to talk, and enjoyed the feeling of trying to be an encourager.

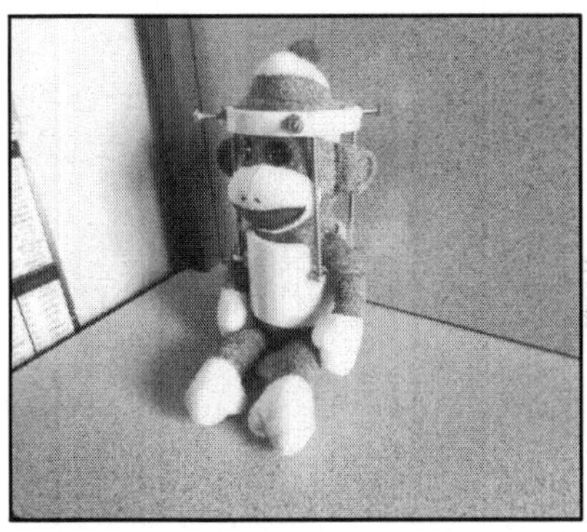

My engineer friend, Bob Williams, brought me this modified sock puppet to encourage me as soon as we got back to Lynchburg. We all agreed the puppet looked just like me, and I named him Buddy Bob.

Say "I Love You" Before It's Too Late

What was it like growing up in your family? Did you tell your siblings or your parents that you loved them from the time you were small? Did your parents and grandparents tell you the same?

In my wife's family they said those words often, from as early as she can remember. Not so in my family. Maybe it was because my family had three sons and Gail's family consisted of two daughters. Some think today that there's no difference between boys and girls, but we didn't believe that back in the '50s—consequently the sexes were treated differently. Generally that was a good thing, but maybe not always.

When I was born my paternal grandfather gave my father some advice: Boys should never be coddled or shown affection. "It makes them weak," he said. As you can imagine, neither my father nor his two brothers ever heard the words "I love you" from their father. My paternal grandmother, although a kind woman in many ways, was nonetheless a product of her generation, and if the phrase "suck it up" had been around then, she would have used it. I remember being told by her on more than one occasion to maintain a stiff upper lip.

That's just the way it was, and I don't feel a compelling need to join a therapy group to uncover any repressed emotional trauma. Growing up, I felt that my parents and both sets of grandparents did love me and my brothers. Later, however, when Gail and I got married, I adopted her habit of saying "I love you." And when our sons were born, both of us used those words from the beginning.

My maternal grandfather died in 1983, and both my paternal grandparents died in 2001. There's something about the finality of death that makes me wish I'd done a few things differently. I should have specifically told them "Thank you for all you've done," I should have recorded more of their stories, and I should have told them I loved them.

After our plane wreck I also felt I should tell my dad that I love him. It's funny how a near-death experience can change your perspective. Dad has softened up some in the past several years, and he's become more emotionally expressive with his youngest grandchildren—and apparently he had been thinking about how he should be doing the same with his grown sons. I guess the accident changed his perspective on a few things too.

Care to guess which of us ended up being the bigger man? You've got a fifty-fifty chance. OK, I'll spare you the drama—it was Dad. To be honest, this still isn't something we say very often or that we're totally comfortable with. Old age will eventually cloud our memories—hopefully his first, but if I keep hitting my head so hard, it might be mine—but at least this is one thing we won't have regrets about.

Having Sons and Daughters-in-Law Who Are Responsible is Better than Gold

At the time of the accident, my son Nathan and his wife Alexandra had been married almost four years, and CJ and Megan (now married) had been dating for over a year. All four of them were more than up to the task of dealing with the confusion, stress, and paperwork of an out-of-state airplane accident. What a blessing to have such great kids!

About two years ago, some friends who had been living in another state returned to Lynchburg after being gone for many years. Our children had been involved in some of the same activities when they were little, but we hadn't been close friends with the parents, so we had not stayed in contact. Gail ran into the wife a few days after their return, and this friend had some sad stories to tell.

Apparently the years had not been good to this couple—their kids had made life miserable. Gail listened as she was told of drug abuse, problems with the law, divorce, failed attempts at education, illegitimate children, and little success at jobs. It was heartbreaking, and I felt bad for them. The reasons for their children's troubled lives could be the subject of another entire book, but this sort of thing happens in all kinds of families—sometimes in very good families.

So if your kids (and their spouses) turn out to be responsible, well adjusted, hard-working, God-honoring, family-oriented, truthful, loving, thrifty, respectful, resourceful, appreciative, caring, confident,

This is our most recent family picture. It caught Gail squinting, and I should have straightened my head, but our kids look great. Left to right: Alexandra, Nate, me, Gail, CJ, and Megan.

kind, dependable, grateful, patriotic, sincere, determined, fair, thorough, creative, self-controlled, committed, trustworthy, generous, organized, diligent, discerning, and considerate of their parents, then you are a fortunate person indeed—and almost as blessed as I am.

Physically Hurting Someone You Love is Worse than Hurting Yourself

Gail tells me that I said at least five or six times, "I am so sorry," as we were hanging upside down in our plane. Do you know why I kept saying that? BECAUSE I WAS SO SORRY! I was panicking at the realization that I had just seriously hurt my wife of thirty-three years. Only eight days earlier we had celebrated our anniversary with dinner at our favorite restaurant.

You know, if I were to ask Gail what we had to eat for our meal that night, she could tell me. How do I know? Because I know *her*, and that's one of many things she easily remembers. She loves to cook, and she loves the cooking channels, so she pays attention to food. Sadly, fine culinary abilities—hers or anyone else's—are sort of wasted on me.

And that's just the first item on a long list of differences between the two of us. We look at just about everything differently, and yes, such dissimilarities can sometimes be a source of contention. But they can also be a source of enjoyment. For example, one of us almost always gets out of bed happy and sings while making breakfast. Guess which one! One of us also loves to talk and will entertain the troops for hours. Care to guess again? Right—not me. Wouldn't our small world—hers and mine—be a terribly boring place if she were just like me?

The extent to which you can get to know someone you've been married to for a long time can be pretty amazing *if you take the time to work at it.* And the thought of physically hurting that person you know so well, and whose life is inextricably woven together with yours, is beyond devastating. Compared to that, pain inflicted on yourself is no big deal.

Causing Emotional Distress to Someone You Love is Pretty Painful, Too

Sorry, Mom and Dad! I know you were anticipating a nice afternoon as you waited at the airport to see Gail and me fly in. The last thing you expected to witness was a plane crash. Surprising how things can go wrong in an instant, and suddenly your life is changed. How can anyone ever prepare for that?

Here's a thought: What about having a reasoned faith in a God who made everything, who loves us, and who tells us that we can live forever with Him when we die? Someone might respond to that type of conviction with words like "crutch" or "opiate of the masses." Doesn't matter. My parents believe it.

I know I caused emotional pain to everyone in our family, but I feel especially bad about hurting my parents. They're not old yet—I refuse to use that word until they reach ninety—but they're not exactly young either, and I thought of them as we were careening off the runway. I didn't want them to see what was happening.

I told Mom several times, when I was in the ER, just how sorry I was, and that was the only time I became emotional. Mothers do hold a special place in your heart, don't they? Funny how the things we learn in those early years stick with us for a lifetime and how a bond is formed between siblings and parents that can never be broken. *Sorry, Dan and Rob.*

Good Neighbors and Friends are Priceless

Where do I even begin to describe all the food? I think I need to call the Food Network and tell them I have an idea for a new cooking-channel program. In it, I would go to the home of everyone who brought us meals and describe in mouth-watering detail every step that went into preparing the main courses and desserts that these good people brought. Church family, neighbors, and friends were all determined that Gail and I were not going to starve. I thought of listing everyone who helped by name, but there were just too many.

Two people that I do have to make special mention of, however, are our immediate neighbors on the east side of our house—Ken and Sharon Moore. Ken is a retired engineer, and Sharon closed her catering business just a few years ago. Yes, I said "catering business" and yes, she was good! We've been neighbors since 1996, and for years our family was one of several local beneficiaries of Sharon's business. She often called to say, "Hey, I made an extra fresh peach pie today; would you like it?" or, "One of my German chocolate cakes fell a little, and I can't use it tomorrow."

Sharon is out of the catering business now, but she hasn't lost a step. Dozens of times over the course of our convalescence the phone would ring and Ken would be on the other end, saying, "Sharon just made [fill in the blank with something really good], and we hope you haven't eaten dinner yet." Then in a few minutes he would walk the short distance between our homes, carrying a full meal (dessert included) that would always be enough for at least two dinners.

Our sincerest "thank you" goes out to Ken, Sharon, and so many others who supported us not only with food but with calls, cards, emails, well-wishes, thoughts, and prayers. It is humbling to be on the receiving end of such an outpouring of love and concern. It's also fattening. I didn't want to admit it, but confession is good for the soul—I put on twenty pounds during the five months I wasn't able to drive. I couldn't exercise, but I could eat, and there were always great desserts around our house.

I've already lost that added weight, but not before I made detailed notes about just who the best bakers are in our crowd. *"Hello, is this the Food Network?"*

Task-Oriented People Often Neglect Everyone but Themselves

Some of us are "people-persons" and some of us are "thing-persons." People-persons are energized by other people and love to be out where the action is. To have to be by themselves is considered absolute torture. Thing-persons, on the other hand, are energized by their projects or their hobbies, and they can never find enough time to spend working on, or playing at, these favorite "things." Crowds drain their energy, and they avoid them whenever possible. Usually these two different people marry one another, and you can always tell which one is which at dinner parties.

I built three different houses for our family and an airplane...Do you think you might know which type of person I am? And those three houses were timber-framed structures that required labor-intensive mortise and tenon work on many pieces of large wood. I spent every evening, every Saturday, and sometimes a few hours on Sunday afternoon working on those homes, and each one took a couple of years. They were fun—but they consumed a lot of time.

The only drawback to enjoying your work as much as I do is that you tend to spend too much time doing it. When our older son, CJ, was about five, he asked Gail if she would divorce me. Gail was shocked and asked why he would ever want her to do that. He replied, "Well, Brandon's parents are divorced and Brandon gets to see his dad on weekends." Out of the mouths of babes. I'm embarrassed to tell that story, and I'm even more embarrassed to admit that it really didn't change my habits much at the time.

I *am* thankful to announce, however, that both our sons turned out to be normal and well-adjusted in spite of my shortcomings. On certain days—such as Father's Day and my birthday, when I get great cards from them—I even want to lay claim to a small measure of responsibility for their success. Nevertheless, I realize that I do need to get out of the shop more often and make a conscious effort to be more of a people-person.

My Sense of Worth and Purpose was Closely—Too Closely—Tied to My Work

I guess that shouldn't come as any great surprise to anyone. You're probably the same way. I started working (mowing lawns for money) when I was ten years old, and hadn't stopped for forty-seven years until the accident. It was actually the sudden interruption of my work that caused all this introspection. It's amazing what you think about when all you *can* do is think.

It's common for men in their mid-fifties to look back at the choices they've made and to look forward with more intensity to the years they have left. I started to do that a year or two before the accident, but the moments of self-analysis were fleeting because I was still racing through life at the busy pace I enjoyed so much.

After taking a harder look at life and work, I reached some conclusions that were less revelation than reaffirmation—a confirmation of things I'd always believed but often failed to practice. Things like (a) work is important, but it usually comes to an end before you do (so don't forget relationships); (b) life is short (everyone's favorite cliché, but now I'm acting more as though I believe it); and (c) the sum total of your value to God, family, and friends goes far beyond your vocation.

There you have it—nothing profound, just a few simple thoughts that I've decided to integrate into my life and not merely acknowledge. I'm not saying that relating yourself closely to your work is necessarily a bad thing, but just that your entire purpose in life should not be determined by your work. I hope to continue doing what I enjoy for a long time yet, but I don't want my entire life to be focused on my work or my projects to the point that I neglect everything and everybody else. I've said several times that the accident was a life-changing event, and this is one of those changes.

Love and Respect are Crucial in a Relationship

How much do I want to tell you about Gail and our thirty-four years of married history? Not much really. We tend to be fairly private people. Maybe if it had been perfect and I wanted to write a book on how to have an exemplary marriage, I would share more. But that's not my purpose.

Neither of us has ever been unfaithful or physically abusive. We've never been hooked on drugs or alcohol. We seldom argued in front of our kids and rarely raised our voices. What we were both guilty of, however, was being first-born children with type-A personalities (read that as "stubborn").

We have polar opposite views on just about everything: How to raise kids, spend money, save stuff, paint walls, deal with people, decorate houses, drive a car, take a vacation, dress, eat in restaurants, do yard work, load the dishwasher, watch television, spend leisure time, organize a closet, walk down the street, sit in a class, talk on the phone, watch a sporting event, go shopping, clean the house, do laundry, travel somewhere, and deal with problems. These are just a *few* of the things we disagree on. We see the world differently in almost every situation.

There's no need to get into the specifics of which one of us does a certain thing one way and which one does it the other—if I did that then you would all be on my side and it wouldn't be fair to Gail (*yeah, right!*). The point is, I wanted things to be done my way—the "correct" way—and Gail tended to do them her way. And because of that, I felt she didn't have any respect for me or my opinions.

Before I go any further and you think I'm a dictatorial tyrant, let me defend myself and ask a question. If a woman could have love or respect, which would she choose? What about a man—what would he choose? You may already know the answers, but for many this comes as a surprise. Almost always, women say they want to be loved, and men say they want to be respected. That's a very important difference between the sexes.

In 2004, Emerson Eggerichs wrote a book entitled *Love & Respect*. On the back cover of the book he summarizes the content by saying: "A wife has one driving need—to feel loved. When that need is met, she is happy. A husband has one driving need—to feel respected. When that need is met, he is happy. When either of these needs isn't met, things get crazy. *Love & Respect* reveals why spouses react negatively to each other, and how they can deal with such conflict."

I couldn't have read this book thirty-four years ago, but as I discovered later, my typically masculine reaction to our conflict—*if she isn't going to respect me, then I'm not going to love her*—was very wrong. My intentional obstinacy started to come out in the first several years of our marriage, and after fifteen or twenty years the battle lines were clearly drawn, and we weren't fighting on the same side. By being distant, neglectful, cold, and unloving I was cutting off my nose to spite my face, and I didn't even care...Anger is seldom rational.

Fortunately for both of us, we had a plane wreck. That sounds stupid, doesn't it? But I'm not being flippant. Although I would never want to go through this experience again—or put my family through it—good things can come out of bad, and that's what happened here. Today I appreciate life more; I appreciate Gail and her strengths more; and I refuse to focus on any of the differences that used to divide us. In a way I could not have anticipated, the plane that was built to shorten distances and bring me closer to the people I love has already accomplished its mission.

You Think a Lot About Praying and Your Relationship to God

Whether you believe in God or not, there's a pretty good chance that if you ever find yourself trying frantically to get out of a wrecked plane, you could suddenly hear yourself calling, *GOD, DON'T LET ME BURN IN THIS DAMN THING!* Maybe that's just me.

Or what if you wore a halo for three months, only to be told that one of the broken vertebrae didn't heal, and you might have to have your neck fused in such a way that your head would never move again? Wouldn't it be nice to have a large number of people praying for your upcoming surgery rather than just having them say, "Sucks to be you, doesn't it?" Yeah, I think so too.

According to the most recent statistics I could find on religion, eighty-four percent of the people in this country believe in God and pray. Roughly seventy-five percent of them are some variety of Christian; the remainder includes Jews, Muslims, Buddhists, Hindus, and adherents of other faiths. In one survey, sixty-four percent of Americans say they pray more than once a day. Apparently a lot of people in this country pray.

But with around sixteen percent of the population not believing in any God, there must be a lot of people who probably consider praying a waste of time. Just this morning as I was organizing my thoughts to start writing about this borrowed insight, I came across a pertinent discussion on a popular plane website.

On the site, a guy was being taken up for his first ride in a small plane, and when the pilot was looking the other direction, this passenger made the sign of the cross. He was obviously nervous. After the flight when the pilot reviewed what was recorded on his GoPro camera, he saw the anxious passenger crossing himself in prayer. It was kind of funny and looked like the neophyte flyer didn't want to offend the pilot, but at the same time he wanted to cover all his bases and invoke the protection of the Almighty.

Several comments were posted on the site, and one in particular caught my attention. Someone responded, "Sorry, but I just don't get this. God, Allah, Buddha, or the Great Spirit lets millions die on a daily basis…I put my faith in a good design, well built with good piloting skills." In one sense, I agree with this fellow, and would much prefer him to be my builder/pilot over another who does his flying on the proverbial "wing and a prayer." But I don't think that's the point here.

It sounds like our non-praying friend is refusing to pray because "God lets millions die on a daily basis." Yes, unfortunately death is part of life, and if word ever got out that we could all avoid dying by simply praying to God, I believe the ranks of those who pray would swell to 100% quicker than you could say ten Hail Marys. Maybe the main purpose of prayer is not to avert sickness, death, or disaster, but to keep us aware that this is an incomprehensible universe full of unimaginable mysteries, and you and I just might *not* be the center of all this cosmic activity.

My reasons for praying and my prayers themselves are fairly simple: I want to acknowledge who God is every day; I want to thank God each day for my life (which includes good things, bad things, and eventually even death); and I want to obey God, who tells me in the Christian Scriptures to pray continually. I think most of us have short memories, and the rigors of daily living can cause us to neglect

God, forget God, and ultimately even blame Him for our difficult circumstances. Perhaps that's why we're commanded to constantly pray.

Occasionally I pray for specific things—I sure wanted my neck to heal without being completely fused—but I'm quick to temper those prayers with the long-term attitude of "not my will, but yours, be done." I never want to become angry or disillusioned with God simply because I prayed, and then blamed Him because I got an outcome that was different from the one I requested.

I believe we are born with a soul that will live forever, and that's why it seems unfair that any of us should ever have to die. We're built for eternity, and death seems incongruous to our design. Trying to reconcile these inner conflicts between life and death, health and sickness (along with attempting to understand our place in the cosmos), might be one reason we need to recognize and acknowledge God every day by praying.

EPILOGUE

Do you know someone with an instinctive ability to do one thing and do it incredibly well? I'm not that guy. Instead, my life and career have been an eclectic mix of avocations and vocations—often in a seemingly disparate array. I do a variety of things, and I do some of them well—not brilliantly, but well.

I've always been an avid reader, and in the course of writing this, my first book, I also read several others. Two of those books made me despair over proffering this one. The first was Laura Hillenbrand's book *Unbroken,* and the second was *Wind, Sand and Stars* by Antoine de Saint-Exupéry. Both are exemplary samples of good prose…I could only wish.

I hope you've enjoyed reading this account of my experiences during the past fourteen months, but you should know that I wrote this more for myself than for anyone else. By chronicling the plane crash, the hospital experiences, and several of the things I've been thinking about, I've been able to find meaning and purpose in the most difficult period of my sheltered life.

That being said, I also want the book to be an encouragement to you. Just as Louis Zamperini found peace and a reason to live during a Billy Graham crusade in 1949, faith, hope, love, and forgiveness from an eternal, all-powerful God can provide stability, purpose, and comfort in your life too. Jesus said, "I am the way, and the truth, and the life." If you don't believe in God, then I'm sorry, and we'll have to agree to disagree—you can leave me alone in my ignorant bliss, and I'll leave you alone in yours. However, if you consider yourself to be an open-minded thinking person who is beginning to consider the existence of God, I would encourage you to read C. S. Lewis's *Mere Christianity*, or possibly *The Case for Christ* by Lee Strobel.

My RV-7A is now back in its hangar at Falwell Airport, and I've flown it four times since it was refurbished. However, I have not flown it by myself yet. Jerry Jackson, a friend and fellow pilot who experienced a crash in January 2013, told me when I saw him at Oshkosh that it takes about three years to shake the residual fears of an accident. Time will tell.

For pilots who have never been to W24 in Lynchburg, Virginia, let me encourage you to come visit sometime and "fly the hill." Just be sure to land on 28 and not on 10. The runway is so steep that they literally use it for soap box derby races in the summer, and you'll never get stopped if you land in the wrong direction. Maybe we'll have a chance to meet there someday.

Until then, I wish you Godspeed, safe landings, and blue skies.

Back at W24

ACKNOWLEDGMENTS

Given that I've waited until my late fifties to write a book, the list of people I should thank for helping me throughout the years could be as lengthy as the book itself. But I'll try to be selective!

Thanks first should go to my parents, Charlie and Beverly Hagerty, who provided a foundation that is still supportive these many years later. My wife Gail merits special mention: After fifteen years of working in higher education, I wanted to venture into the world of self-employment, and Gail encouraged me to take what was for us at that time a very big step. She's also been the one to stand behind a few other risky business ideas and to allow me the freedom to complete several long-term projects. Who wouldn't be thankful for that kind of support over the course of thirty-four years? I think we make a pretty good team. I've already bragged about my sons and daughters-in-law throughout the book, but this is a special thank-you to CJ, Nathan, Alexandra, and Megan for their encouragement and sacrifice during a most difficult time.

All of the medical professionals who cared for Gail and me are deserving of our sincerest gratitude, but special appreciation is reserved for Dr. Jim Maserati and Dr. Hugh Gill and the skills they exhibited in the operating room. Their specialized abilities make a difference in people's lives every day.

The staff at Morris Publishing provided several invaluable services that enabled this book to be completed. Their abilities, along with the proofreading talents and sage advice of Carol Champagne and Gary Wooldridge, helped to shape the content and make it more readable.

Finally, special thanks are due to Kathy Shaibani for her skillful editing and guidance throughout the writing process. Her ability to manipulate the written word and her attention to detail are talents that have been polished while working through many manuscripts, and I have been the beneficiary of those years of experience.

Chuck Hagerty
November 2014